TEACHER'S PET PUBLICATIONS

LITPLAN TEACHER PACK
for
Much Ado About Nothing
based on the play by
William Shakespeare

Written by
Susan R. Woodward

© 2007 Teacher's Pet Publications
All Rights Reserved

This **LitPlan** for
Much Ado About Nothing
has been brought to you by Teacher's Pet Publications, Inc.

Copyright Teacher's Pet Publications 2007

Only the student materials in this unit plan (such as worksheets, study questions, and tests) may be reproduced multiple times for use in the purchaser's classroom.

For any additional copyright questions, contact Teacher's Pet Publications.

www.tpet.com

TABLE OF CONTENTS - *Much Ado About Nothing*

Introduction	10
Unit Objective	12
Reading Assignment Sheet	13
Unit Outline	14
Study Questions (Short Answer)	17
Quiz/Study Questions (Multiple Choice)	29
Pre-reading Vocabulary Worksheets	49
Lesson One (Introductory Lesson)	73
Nonfiction Assignment Sheet	81
Oral Reading Evaluation Form	85
Peer Performance Feedback Sheet	86
Writing Assignment 1 (Creative)	89
Writing Assignment 2 (Informative)	94
Writing Evaluation Form	95
Writing Assignment 3 (Persuasive)	113
Peer Edit Form	115
Vocabulary Review Activities	107
Extra Writing Assignments/Discussion ?s	109
Group Presentation Evaluation Form	118
Unit Review Activities	119
WebQuest (Electronic Enrichment)	121
Unit Tests	129
Unit Resource Materials	177
Vocabulary Resource Materials	195

ABOUT THE AUTHOR
WILLIAM SHAKESPEARE

SHAKESPEARE, William (1564-1616). For more than 350 years, William Shakespeare has been the world's most popular playwright. On the stage, in the movies, and on television his plays are watched by vast audiences. People read his plays again and again for pleasure. Students reading his plays for the first time are delighted by what they find.

Shakespeare's continued popularity is due to many things. His plays are filled with action, his characters are believable, and his language is thrilling to hear or read. Underlying all this is Shakespeare's deep humanity. He was a profound student of people and he understood them. He had a great tolerance, sympathy, and love for all people, good or evil.

While watching a Shakespearean tragedy, the audience is moved and shaken. After the show the spectators are calm, washed clean of pity and terror. They are saddened but at peace, repeating the old saying, "There, but for the grace of God, go I."

A Shakespearean comedy is full of fun. The characters are lively; the dialogue is witty. In the end young lovers are wed; old babblers are silenced; wise men are content. The comedies are joyous and romantic.

Boyhood in Stratford

William Shakespeare was born in Stratford-upon-Avon, England, in 1564. This was the sixth year of the reign of Queen Elizabeth I. He was christened on April 26 of that year. The day of his birth is unknown. It has long been celebrated on April 23, the feast of St. George.

He was the third child and oldest son of John and Mary Arden Shakespeare. Two sisters, Joan and Margaret, died before he was born. The other children were Gilbert, a second Joan, Anne, Richard, and Edmund. Only the second Joan outlived William.

Shakespeare's father was a tanner and glovemaker. He was an alderman of Stratford for years. He also served a term as high bailiff, or mayor. Toward the end of his life John Shakespeare lost most of his money. When he died in 1601, he left William only a little real estate. Not much is known about Mary Shakespeare, except that she came from a wealthier family than her husband.

Stratford-upon-Avon is in Warwickshire, called the heart of England. In Shakespeare's day it was well farmed and heavily wooded. The town itself was prosperous and progressive.

The town was proud of its grammar school. Young Shakespeare went to it, although when or for how long is not known. He may have been a pupil there between his 7th and 13th years. His studies must have been mainly in Latin. The schooling was good. All four schoolmasters at the school during Shakespeare's boyhood were graduates of Oxford University.

Nothing definite is known about his boyhood. From the content of his plays, he must have learned early about the woods and fields, about birds, insects, and small animals, about trades and outdoor sports, and about the country people he later portrayed with such good humor. Then and later he picked up an amazing stock of facts about hunting, hawking, fishing, dances, music, and other arts and sports. Among other subjects, he also learned about alchemy, astrology, folklore, medicine, and law. As good writers do, he collected information both from books and from daily observation of the world around him.

Marriage and Life in London

In 1582, when he was 18, he married Anne Hathaway. She was from Shottery, a village a mile from Stratford. Anne was seven or eight years older than Shakespeare. From this difference in their ages, a story arose that they were unhappy together. Their first daughter, Susanna, was born in 1583. In 1585 a twin boy and girl, Hamnet and Judith, were born.

What Shakespeare did between 1583 and 1592 is not known. Various stories are told. He may have taught school, worked in a lawyer's office, served on a rich man's estate, or traveled with a company of actors. One famous story says that about 1584 he and some friends were caught poaching on the estate of Sir Thomas Lucy of Carlecote, near Warwick, and were forced to leave town. A less likely story is that he was in London in 1588. There he was supposed to have held horses for theater patrons and later to have worked in the theaters as a callboy.

By 1592, however, Shakespeare was definitely in London and was already recognized as an actor and playwright. He was then 28 years old. In that year he was referred to in another man's book for the first time. Robert Greene, a playwright, accused him of borrowing from the plays of others.

Between 1592 and 1594, plague kept the London theaters closed most of the time. During these years Shakespeare wrote his earliest sonnets and two long narrative poems, 'Venus and Adonis' and 'The Rape of Lucrece'. Both were printed by Richard Field, a boyhood friend from Stratford. They were well received and helped establish him as a poet.

Shakespeare Prospers

Until 1598 Shakespeare's theater work was confined to a district northeast of London. This was outside the walls, in the parish of Shoreditch. Located there were two playhouses, the Theatre and the Curtain. Both were managed by James Burbage, whose son Richard Burbage was Shakespeare's friend and the greatest tragic actor of his day.

Up to 1596 Shakespeare lived near these theaters in Bishopsgate, where the North Road entered the city. Sometime between 1596 and 1599, he moved across the Thames River to a district called Bankside. There, two theaters, the Rose and the Swan, had been built by Philip Henslowe. He was James Burbage's chief competitor in London as a theater manager.

The Burbages also moved to this district in 1598 and built the famous Globe Theatre. Its sign showed Atlas supporting the world-hence the theater's name. Shakespeare was associated with the Globe Theatre for the rest of his active life. He owned shares in it, which brought him much money.

Meanwhile, in 1597, Shakespeare had bought New Place, the largest house in Stratford. During the next three years he bought other property in Stratford and in London. The year before, his father, probably at Shakespeare's suggestion, applied for and was granted a coat of arms. It bore the motto Non sanz droict-Not without right. From this time on, Shakespeare could write "Gentleman" after his name. This meant much to him, for in his day actors were classed legally with criminals and vagrants.

Shakespeare's name first appeared on the title pages of his printed plays in 1598. In the same year Francis Meres, in 'Palladis Tamia: Wit's Treasury', praised him as a poet and dramatist. Meres's comments on 12 of Shakespeare's plays showed that Shakespeare's genius was recognized in his own time.

Honored As Actor and Playwright

Queen Elizabeth I died in 1603. King James I followed her to the throne. Shakespeare's theatrical company was taken under the king's patronage and called the King's Company. Shakespeare and the other actors were made officers of the royal household. The theatrical company was the most successful of its time. Before it was the King's Company, it had been known as the Earl of Derby's and the Lord Chamberlain's. In 1608 the company acquired the Blackfriars Theatre. This was a smaller and more aristocratic theater than the Globe. Thereafter the company alternated between the two playhouses.

Plays by Shakespeare were performed at both theaters, at the royal court, and in the castles of the nobles. After 1603 Shakespeare probably acted little, although he was still a good actor. His favorite roles seem to have been old Adam in 'As You Like It' and the Ghost in 'Hamlet'.

In 1607, when he was 43, he may have suffered a serious physical breakdown. In the same year his older daughter Susanna married John Hall, a doctor. The next year Shakespeare's first grandchild, Elizabeth, was born. Also in 1607 his brother Edmund, who had been an actor in London, died at the age of 27.

The Mermaid Tavern Group

About this time Shakespeare became one of the group of now-famous writers who gathered at the Mermaid Tavern in Cheapside. The club was formed by Sir Walter Raleigh. Ben Jonson was its leading spirit (see Jonson). Shakespeare was a popular member. He was admired for his talent and loved for his kindliness. Thomas Fuller, writing about 50 years later, gave an amusing account of the conversational duels between Shakespeare and Jonson:

"Many were the wit-combats betwixt him and Ben Jonson; which two I behold like a Spanish great galleon and an English man-of-war; Master Jonson (like the former) was built far higher in learning; solid, but slow, in his performances. Shakespeare, with the English man-of-war, lesser in bulk, but lighter in sailing, could turn with all tides, tack about, and take advantage of all winds, by the quickness of his wit and invention."

Jonson sometimes criticized Shakespeare harshly. Nevertheless he later wrote a eulogy of Shakespeare that is remarkable for its feeling and acuteness. In it he said:

> Leave thee alone, for the comparison
> Of all that insolent Greece or haughty Rome
> Sent forth, or since did from their ashes come.
> Triumph, my Britain, thou hast one to show
> To whom all scenes of Europe homage owe.
> He was not of an age, but for all time!
> . . . .
> Sweet Swan of Avon! what a sight it were
> To see thee in our waters yet appear,
> And make those flights upon the banks of Thames,
> That so did take Eliza, and our James!

Death and Burial at Stratford

Shakespeare retired from his theater work in 1610 and returned to Stratford. His friends from London visited him. In 1613 the Globe Theatre burned. He lost much money in it, but he was still wealthy. He shared in the building of the new Globe. A few months before the fire he bought as an investment a house in the fashionable Blackfriars district of London.

On April 23, 1616, Shakespeare died at the age of 52. This date is according to the Old Style, or Julian, calendar of his time. The New Style, or Gregorian, calendar date is May 3, 1616. He was buried in the chancel of the Church of the Holy Trinity in Stratford.

A stone slab-a reproduction of the original one, which it replaced in 1830-marks his grave. It bears an inscription, perhaps written by himself.

On the north wall of the chancel is his monument. It consists of a portrait bust enclosed in a stone frame. Below it is an inscription in Latin and English. This bust and the engraving by Martin Droeshout, prefixed to the First Folio edition of his plays (1623), are the only pictures of Shakespeare which can be accepted as showing his true likeness.

John Aubrey, an English antiquarian, wrote about Shakespeare 65 years after the poet's death. He evidently used information furnished by the son of one of Shakespeare's fellow actors. Aubrey described him as "a handsome, well-shaped man, very good company, and of a ready and pleasant smooth wit."

Shakespeare's will, still in existence, bequeathed most of his property to Susanna and her daughter. He left small mementoes to friends. He mentioned his wife only once, leaving her his "second best bed" with its furnishings.

Much has been written about this odd bequest. There is little reason to think it was a slight. Indeed, it may have been a special mark of affection. The "second best bed" was probably the one they used. The best bed was reserved for guests. At any rate, his wife was entitled by law to one third of her husband's goods and real estate and to the use of their home for life. She died in 1623.

The will contains three signatures of Shakespeare. These, with three others, are the only known specimens of his handwriting in existence. Several experts also regard some lines in the manuscript of 'Sir Thomas More' as Shakespeare's own handwriting. He spelled his name in various ways. His father's papers show about 16 spellings. Shakspere, Shaxpere, and Shakespeare are the most common.

Did Shakespeare Really Write the Plays?

The outward events of Shakespeare's life are ordinary. He was hard-working, sober, and middle-class in his ways. He steadily gathered wealth and took good care of his family. Many people have found it impossible to believe that such a man could have written the plays. They feel that he could not have known such heights and depths of passion. They believe that the people around Shakespeare expressed little realization of his greatness. Some say that a man of his little schooling could not have learned about the professions, the aristocratic sports of hawking and hunting, the speech and manners of the upper classes.

Since the 1800's there has been a steady effort to prove that Shakespeare did not write the plays or that others did. For a long time the leading candidate was Sir Francis Bacon. Books on the Shakespeare-Bacon argument would fill a library (see Bacon, Francis). After Bacon became less popular, the Earl of Oxford and then other men were suggested as the authors. Nearly every famous Elizabethan was named. The most recent has been Christopher Marlowe. Some people even claim that "Shakespeare" is an assumed name for a whole group of poets and playwrights.

However, some men around Shakespeare-for example, Meres in 1598 and Jonson in 1623-did recognize his worth as a man and as a writer. To argue that an obscure Stratford boy could not have become the Shakespeare of literature is to ignore the mystery of genius. His knowledge is of the kind that could not be learned in school. It is the kind that only a genius could learn, by applying a keen intelligence to everyday life. Some great writers have had even less schooling than Shakespeare.

Few scholars take seriously these attempts to deprive Shakespeare of credit. Shakespeare's style is individual and cannot be imitated. Any good student recognizes it. It can be found nowhere else. Bacon is a poor candidate for the honor. Great as he was, he was certainly not a poet.

How the Plays Came Down to Us

Since the 1700's scholars have worked over the text of Shakespeare's plays. They have had to do so because the plays were badly printed, and no original manuscripts of them survive.

In Shakespeare's day plays were not usually printed under the author's supervision. When a playwright sold a play to his company, he lost all rights to it. He could not sell it again to a publisher without the company's consent. When the play was no longer in demand on the stage, the company itself might sell the manuscript. Plays were eagerly read by the Elizabethan public. This was even more true during the plague years, when the theaters were closed. It was also true during times of business depression. Sometimes plays were taken down in shorthand and sold. At other times, a dismissed actor would write down the play from memory and sell it.

About half of Shakespeare's plays were printed during his lifetime in small, cheap pamphlets called quartos. Most of these were made from fairly accurate manuscripts. A few were in garbled form.

In 1623, seven years after Shakespeare's death, his collected plays were published in a large, expensive volume called the First Folio. It contains all his plays except two of which he wrote only part-'Pericles' and 'Two Noble Kinsmen'. It also has the first engraved portrait of Shakespeare.

This edition was authorized by Shakespeare's acting group, the King's Company. Some of the plays in it were printed from the accurate quartos and some from manuscripts in the theater. It is certain that many of these manuscripts were in Shakespeare's own handwriting. Others were copies. Still others, like the 'Macbeth' manuscript, had been revised by another dramatist.

Shakespearean scholars have been determining what Shakespeare actually wrote. They have done so by studying the language, stagecraft, handwriting, and printing of the period and by carefully examining and comparing the different editions. They have modernized spelling and punctuation, supplied stage directions, explained difficult passages, and made the plays easier for the modern reader to understand.

Another hard task has been to find out when the plays were written. About half of them have no definite date of composition. The plays themselves have been searched for clues. Other books have been examined. Scholars have tried to match events in Shakespeare's life with the subject matter of his plays.

These scholars have used detective methods. They have worked with clues, deduction, shrewd reasoning, and external and internal evidence. External evidence consists of actual references in other books. Internal evidence is made up of verse tests and a study of the poet's imagery and figures of speech, which changed from year to year.

The verse tests follow the idea that a poet becomes more skillful with practice. Scholars long ago noticed that in his early plays Shakespeare used little prose, much rhyme, and certain types of rhythmical and metrical regularity. As he grew older he used more prose, less rhyme, and greater freedom and variety in rhythm and meter. From these facts, scholars have figured out the dates of those plays that had none.

Shakespeare As a Dramatist

The facts about Shakespeare are interesting in themselves, but they have little to do with his place in literature. Shakespeare wrote his plays to give pleasure. It is possible to spoil that pleasure by giving too much attention to his life, his times, and the problem of figuring out what he actually wrote. He can be enjoyed in book form, in the theater, or on television without our knowing any of these things.

Some difficulties stand in the way of this enjoyment. Shakespeare wrote more than 350 years ago. The language he used is naturally somewhat different from the language of today. Besides, he wrote in verse. Verse permits a free use of words that may not be understood by some readers. His plays are often fanciful. This may not appeal to matter-of-fact people who are used to modern realism. For all these reasons, readers may find him difficult. The worst handicap to enjoyment is the notion that Shakespeare is a "classic," a writer to be approached with awe.

The way to escape this last difficulty is to remember that Shakespeare wrote his plays for everyday people and that many in the audience were uneducated. They looked upon him as a funny, exciting, and lovable entertainer, not as a great poet. People today should read him as the people in his day listened to him. The excitement and enjoyment of the plays will banish most of the difficulties.

--- Courtesy of Compton's Learning Company

INTRODUCTION

This LitPlan has been designed to develop students' reading, writing, thinking, and language skills through exercises and activities related to *Much Ado About Nothing*. It includes twenty-one lessons, supported by extra resource materials.

The **introductory lesson** introduces students to Shakespearean language. Following the introductory activity, students are given a transition to explain how the activity relates to the play they are about to read. Following the transition, students are given the materials they will be using during the unit. At the end of the lesson, students begin the pre-reading work for the first reading assignment.

The **reading assignments** are approximately thirty pages each; some are a little shorter while others are a little longer. Students have approximately 15 minutes of pre-reading work to do prior to each reading assignment. This pre-reading work involves reviewing the study questions for the assignment and doing some vocabulary work for 7 to10 vocabulary words they will encounter in their reading.

The **study guide questions** are fact-based questions; students can find the answers to these questions right in the text. These questions come in two formats: short answer or multiple choice. The best use of these materials is probably to use the short answer version of the questions as study guides for students (since answers will be more complete), and to use the multiple choice version for occasional quizzes.

The **vocabulary work** is intended to enrich students' vocabularies as well as to aid in the students' understanding of the play. Prior to each reading assignment, students will complete a two-part worksheet for 7 to 10 vocabulary words in the upcoming reading assignment. Part I focuses on students' use of general knowledge and contextual clues by giving the sentence in which the word appears in the text. Students are then to write down what they think the words mean based on the words' usage. Part II nails down the definitions of the words by giving students dictionary definitions of the words and having students match the words to the correct definitions based on the words' contextual usage. Students should then have an understanding of the words when they meet them in the text.

After each reading assignment, students will go back and formulate answers for the study guide questions. Discussion of these questions serves as a **review** of the most important events and ideas presented in the reading assignments.

After students complete reading the work, there is a **vocabulary review** lesson which pulls together all of the fragmented vocabulary lists for the reading assignments and gives students a review of all of the words they have studied.

Following the vocabulary review, a lesson is devoted to the **extra discussion questions/writing assignments**. These questions focus on interpretation, critical analysis and personal response, employing a variety of thinking skills and adding to the students' understanding of the play.

There is a **group theme project** (also one of the required writing assignments for this unit). Student groups will write a three act play based on the format of Shakespearean comedies. Each group will create a plot that follows the standard "boy meets girl, boy loses girl, boy gets girl back" and includes certain stereotypical characters. The groups will rehearse and present their plays at the end of the unit.

There are three **writing assignments** in this unit, each with the purpose of informing, persuading, or having students express personal opinions.
1. The return of Charles II and his changes in the Theatre (informative)
2. Happily ever after? (persuasive)
3. Writing a three act comedy (creative)

There is a **nonfiction reading assignment**. Students must read nonfiction articles, books, etc. to gather information about William Shakespeare's life and the Elizabethan theatre.

The **review lesson** pulls together all of the aspects of the unit. The teacher is given four or five choices of activities or games to use which all serve the same basic function of reviewing all of the information presented in the unit.

The **unit test** comes in two formats: multiple choice or short answer. As a convenience, two different tests for each format have been included. There is also an advanced short answer unit test for advanced students.

There are additional **support materials** included with this unit. The **Unit Resource Materials** section includes suggestions for an in-class library, crossword and word search puzzles related to the play, and extra worksheets. There is a list of **bulletin board ideas** which gives the teacher suggestions for bulletin boards to go along with this unit. In addition, there is a list of **extra class activities** the teacher could choose from to enhance the unit or as a substitution for an exercise the teacher might feel is inappropriate for his/her class. **Answer keys** are located directly after the **reproducible student materials** throughout the unit. The **Vocabulary Resource Materials** section includes similar worksheets and games to reinforce the vocabulary words.

The **Electronic Enrichment** section **(NEW)** allows for collaborative work using the internet and creating a series of projects.

The **level** of this unit can be varied depending upon the criteria on which the individual assignments are graded, the teacher's expectations of his/her students in class discussions, and the formats chosen for the study guides, quizzes and test. If teachers have other ideas/activities they wish to use, they can usually easily be inserted prior to the review lesson.

The student materials may be reproduced for use in the teacher's classroom without infringement of copyrights. No other portion of this unit may be reproduced without the written consent of Teacher's Pet Publications, Inc.

UNIT OBJECTIVES - *Much Ado About Nothing*

1. Through reading William Shakespeare's *Much Ado About Nothing*, students will explore the Bard's world as well as learning some history of Elizabethan theatre and the changes that came with the return of Charles II to the throne. Students will have the opportunity to write their own comedy following the format of Shakespeare's plays.

2. Students will demonstrate their understanding of the text on four levels: factual, interpretive, critical and personal.

3. Students will learn to work cooperatively as well as independently throughout the unit.

4. Students will be given the opportunity to practice reading aloud (performing!) and silently to improve their skills in each area.

5. Students will answer questions to demonstrate their knowledge and understanding of the main events and characters in *Much Ado About Nothing* as they relate to the author's theme development (gender roles in Elizabethan England, appearance vs. reality, love vs. infatuation).

6. Students will enrich their vocabularies and improve their understanding of the play through the vocabulary lessons prepared for use in conjunction with the work.

7. The writing assignments in this unit are geared to several purposes:
    a. To have students demonstrate their abilities to inform, to persuade, or to express their own personal ideas
       Note: Students will demonstrate ability to write effectively to <u>inform</u> by developing and organizing facts to convey information. Students will demonstrate the ability to write effectively to <u>persuade</u> by selecting and organizing relevant information, establishing an argumentative purpose, and by designing an appropriate strategy for an identified audience. Students will demonstrate the ability to write effectively to <u>express personal ideas</u> by selecting a form and its appropriate elements.
    b. To check the students' reading comprehension
    c. To make students think about the ideas presented by the play
    d. To encourage logical thinking
    e. To provide an opportunity to practice good grammar and improve students' use of the English language.

8. Students will read aloud, report, and participate in large and small group discussions to improve their public speaking and personal interaction skills.

READING ASSIGNMENT SHEET - *Much Ado About Nothing*

Date Assigned	Scenes Assigned	Date Completed
	Act I, scene i	
	Act I, scenes ii and iii	
	Act II, scene i	
	Act II, scenes ii and iii	
	Act III, scenes i and ii	
	Act III, scenes iii through v	
	Act IV, scene i	
	Act IV, scene ii	
	Act V, sc. i	
	Act V, scenes ii through iv	

UNIT OUTLINE – *Much Ado About Nothing*

1	2	3	4	5
Intro to Shakespeare's Language PVR Act I, scene i	Study ?s Act I, scene i Media Center Visit: PVR Act I, scenes ii and iii	Study ?s Act I, scenes ii and iii Quiz Act I Read Aloud PVR Act II, scene i	Study ?s Act II, scene i Writing Assignment 1 PVR Act II, scenes ii and iii	Study ?s Act II, scenes ii and iii Quiz Act II Read aloud PVR Act III, scenes ii and iii
6	**7**	**8**	**9**	**10**
Study ?s Act III, scenes ii and iii Group Work: Creative Project continued PVR Act III, scenes iii - v	Study ?s Act III, scenes iii - v Quiz Act III Read aloud PVR Act IV, scene i	Study ?s Act IV, scene i Library/Media Writing Assignment 2 PVR Act IV, scene ii	Study ?s Act IV, scene ii Quiz Act IV Read aloud PVR Act V, scene i	Study ?s Act V, scene i Shakespearean Songs/Poems (creativeproject) PVR Act V, scenes ii - iv
11	**12**	**13**	**14**	**15**
Study ?s Act V, scenes ii - iv Quiz Act V Read aloud	Group Work: Creative Project (continued) the role of the clown	Vocabulary Work	Group Work: Extra Discussion Questions	Group Work: Rehearsals for Creative Project
16	**17**	**18**	**19**	**20**
In-Class Writing: Persuasive	Peer Editing: Persuasive Writing	Performance Day 1	Performance Day 2	Review Materials
21				
Unit Test				

Key: P = Preview Study Questions   V = Vocabulary Work   R= Read

STUDY GUIDE QUESTIONS

SHORT ANSWER STUDY GUIDE QUESTIONS - *Much Ado About Nothing*

Act I, scene i:
1. The messenger tells Leonato someone will be arriving in Messina. Who is coming?
2. Beatrice questions the messenger about someone. Who?
3. According to Leonato, who is fighting a "merry war?"
4. Describe Beatrice's greeting to Benedick upon his arrival.
5. How long do Don Pedro and his company plan on staying in Messina?
6. Who is Don John?
7. Who catches Claudio's eye?
8. What is it that Benedick swears will never happen to him?
9. Where does Claudio say he has spent time before coming to Messina?
10. What does Don Pedro intend to do for Claudio?

Act I, scenes ii and iii:
1. Who is Antonio?
2. What does Antonio claim to have learned from one of his servants?
3. What is Leonato's reaction to the news regarding Don Pedro's wooing his daughter?
4. What are Don John's true feelings toward his brother, Don Pedro?
5. Who is Borachio?
6. What news does Borachio bring to Don John?
7. What does Don John plan to do regarding Claudio and Hero? Why?

Act II, scene i:
1. Who does Leonato notice is not at supper that evening?
2. For what does Beatrice say she is thankful to God every night?
3. Where does Beatrice say that, as an unmarried woman, she shall go?
4. What kind of party is Leonato hosting?
5. How does Beatrice further insult Benedick at Leonato's masquerade party?
6. How does Don John feed false information to Claudio?
7. Who does Claudio become angry with after Don John shares what he has "heard?"
8. What hint does Beatrice drop about the possible reason for her treatment of Benedick?
9. What news does Don Pedro bring to Claudio?
10. What plan does Don Pedro begin to concoct?

Act II, scenes ii and iii:
1. What plan does Borachio devise that pleases Don John?
2. What does Don John promise Borachio if he is able to pull off his scheme?
3. What information does Don John say he is going to obtain?
4. Why does Benedick send a servant to retrieve a book from his room?
5. What changes in Claudio's behavior does Benedick notice?
6. What does Benedick blame for the unfavorable changes he sees in Claudio?
7. What qualities must a woman possess before Benedick will even consider her for a wife?
8. What story do Don Pedro, Balthasar, and Claudio tell while Benedick is hiding in the arbor?

Much Ado About Nothing Study Questions page 2

Act II, scenes ii and iii continued:
9. What knowledge do Don Pedro, Balthasar, and Claudio have that Benedick is not aware of?
10. What is Benedick's reaction to the news he overhears?

Act III, scenes i and ii:
1. What plan have Hero, Margaret, and Ursula agreed to participate in?
2. Why does Hero claim that she will never tell Beatrice of Benedick's "affections?"
3. What is Beatrice's reaction to what she overhears?
4. Where is Don Pedro headed after Claudio and Hero's wedding?
5. What excuse does Benedick give for his melancholy behavior?
6. What do Don Pedro and Claudio claim is "wrong" with Benedick?
7. What changes has Benedick made to his physical appearance?
8. What false news does Don John bring to Don Pedro and Claudio?
9. How does Don John intend to "prove" his accusations?
10. What does Claudio intend to do if he finds out that Hero truly is inappropriately seeing other men?

Act III, scenes iii, iv, and v:
1. Who is Dogberry?
2. What does the reader notice about Dogberry's and Verges's speeches?
3. How does Dogberry instruct his watchmen to deal with any wrongdoers they may encounter?
4. What do the watchmen happen to overhear?
5. Describe Beatrice's mood during the scene with Hero and Margaret. To what does Hero contribute this mood?
6. Describe the verbal banter among the women as they prepare for the wedding.
7. What does Dogberry tell Leonato right before the wedding and what is Leonato's reply?

Act IV, scene i:
1. What is Claudio's response when the Friar asks if he comes to be married?
2. What does Claudio call Hero?
3. What is Claudio's accusation against Hero?
4. How does Hero react to Count Claudio's claims?
5. Describe Leonato's reaction to the Count's accusations.
6. Who defends Hero by saying that her blushes were from embarrassment and not from shame?
7. Who does Benedick suspect is behind the confusion surrounding Hero?
8. Describe the plan that the Friar creates regarding Hero.
9. What confession does Beatrice make to Benedick?
10. What request does Beatrice make of Benedick?

Act IV, scene ii:
1. Of what crimes does Dogberry accuse Borachio and Conrad?
2. What does Don John do after Hero is accused?
3. What does the Sexton suggest that Dogberry do with his prisoners?
4. For what "virtues" does Dogberry claim that he should be respected?

Much Ado About Nothing Study Questions page 3

Act V, scene i:
1. What advice does Antonio give his brother regarding his grief?
2. Why does Leonato challenge Claudio to a duel?
3. How does Antonio defend Leonato?
4. Why does Benedick also challenge Claudio?
5. How does Don Pedro attempt to diffuse the situation between Claudio and Benedick?
6. What news does Claudio learn from Borachio?
7. What does Claudio claim is his only sin in the events surrounding Hero's "death?"
8. What things does Leonato insist that Claudio do in order to restore his daughter Hero's honor?

Act V, scenes ii, iii, and iv:

1. Why does Beatrice want to know what has happened between Benedick and Claudio?
2. What does Claudio do at Hero's tomb?
3. Who sings a hymn at Hero's tomb in her honor?
4. Who does Leonato claim were completely innocent in the accusations about Hero?
5. Besides Don John, who does Leonato decide is also partly to blame for what happened to his daughter?
6. What does Leonato instruct Hero, Margaret, Ursula, and Beatrice to do when Claudio arrives for the wedding ceremony?
7. How does Don Pedro describe Benedick's expression when he and Claudio enter?
8. What does Claudio discover once the wedding party enters?
9. What "evidence" do Claudio and Hero produce as proof that Benedick and Beatrice love each other?

ANSWER KEY SHORT ANSWER STUDY GUIDE QUESTIONS - *Much Ado About Nothing*

Act I, scene i:

1. The messenger tells Leonato someone will be arriving in Messina. Who is coming?
    Don Pedro of Aragon is coming with Count Claudio, Signior Benedick and Don John.

2. Beatrice questions the messenger about someone. Who?
    Beatrice questions the messenger about Signior Benedick.

3. According to Leonato, who is fighting a "merry war?"
    Beatrice and Benedick continuously bicker whenever they are in each other's company. This is the "merry war" that Leonato refers to.

4. Describe Beatrice's greeting to Benedick upon his arrival.
    Beatrice immediately begins to insult him and he banters back.

5. How long do Don Pedro and his company plan on staying in Messina?
    He and his company plan on staying in Messina for one month.

6. Who is Don John?
    Don John is Don Pedro's villainous brother who has recently been reconciled to Don Pedro.

7. Who catches Claudio's eye?
    Leonato's daughter, Hero, catches the eye of the young Count.

8. What is it that Benedick swears will never happen to him?
    Benedick swears that he will never fall in love and marry.

9. Where does Claudio say he has spent time before coming to Messina?
    Claudio has been fighting in a war. Now that the war is over, he is ready to think about love.

10. What does Don Pedro intend to do for Claudio?
    Since Claudio seems to be too shy to speak to Hero on his own behalf, Don Pedro says that he will, at a masked ball, pretend to be Claudio and woo Hero for him.

Act I, scenes ii and iii:

1. Who is Antonio?
    He is Leonato's brother and uncle to Hero and Beatrice.

2. What does Antonio claim to have learned from one of his servants?
   Antonio claims that one of his servants overheard that Don Pedro will woo Leonato's daughter, Hero.

3. What is Leonato's reaction to the news regarding Don Pedro's wooing his daughter?
   He seems to be delighted that the Prince will be wooing his daughter, and he decides to share the news with Hero so that she might prepare an answer.

4. What are Don John's true feelings toward his brother, Don Pedro?
   Don John resents his brother. Don John had gone against Don Pedro in a battle and lost. Don Pedro captured Don John and "reconciled" with him.

5. Who is Borachio?
   Borachio is one of Don John's seedy companions.

6. What news does Borachio bring to Don John?
   Borachio tells Don John that he has learned that Don Pedro will woo Hero (in disguise) for Claudio at the masked ball.

7. What does Don John plan to do regarding Claudio and Hero? Why?
   Don John resents Claudio, and he hopes to ruin Claudio's relationship with Don Pedro by foiling the plans surrounding Hero.

Act II, scene i:

1. Who does Leonato notice is not at supper that evening?
   Leonato notices that Don John is not at supper that night.

2. For what does Beatrice say she is thankful to God every night?
   She says that she is thankful that she has no husband, and that she does not want to marry.

3. Where does Beatrice say that, as an unmarried woman, she shall go?
   In Shakespeare's day, it was believed that all unmarried women go to the gates of hell upon death, so that is where Beatrice says she will find herself when she passes.

4. What kind of party is Leonato hosting?
   Leonato is hosting a masquerade party. This will lead to the ensuing confusion in the play.

5. How does Beatrice further insult Benedick at Leonato's masquerade party?
   While dancing with a masked man, and not knowing that he is Benedick, Beatrice begins to talk negatively about Benedick all the more.

6. How does Don John feed false information to Claudio?
    Don John tells a masked Claudio – Don John knows it is Claudio even though Claudio claims to be Signior Benedick– that Don Pedro is wooing the fair Hero for himself. This makes Claudio angry because Don Pedro had promised to woo Hero for him.

7. Who does Claudio become angry with after Don John shares what he has "heard?"
    Claudio has the audacity to blame Hero for Don Pedro's "wooing" because "beauty is a witch." She must have bewitched Don Pedro to betray Claudio.

8. What hint does Beatrice drop about the possible reason for her treatment of Benedick?
    When speaking of Benedick, she admits that he lent his heart to her for a while, but he hurt her.

9. What news does Don Pedro bring to Claudio?
    Don Pedro tells Claudio that he has won Hero's hand in marriage for Claudio. Claudio now changes his attitude about Hero and becomes a happy groom-to-be.

10. What plan does Don Pedro begin to concoct?
    Don Pedro plots to bring Beatrice and Benedick together.

Act II, scenes ii and iii:

1. What plan does Borachio devise that pleases Don John?
    Borachio tells Don John that he will "visit" Margaret in the night and manage to get them both near a window where Don John will attempt to "prove" to Claudio that Hero is unfaithful. Don John will make both Don Pedro and Claudio believe that it is Hero at the window with Borachio and not Margaret.

2. What does Don John promise Borachio if he is able to pull off his scheme?
    Don John will give Borachio one thousand ducats if he is successful.

3. What information does Don John say he is going to obtain?
    Don John intends to learn the date of Claudio and Hero's wedding so that the plan can be put in motion.

4. Why does Benedick send a servant to retrieve a book from his room?
    Benedick wants to be alone with his brooding about Claudio.

5. What changes in Claudio's behavior does Benedick notice?
    Benedick notices that instead of war drums and the fife, the valiant soldier Claudio now seems to prefer chamber music. He says that at one time Claudio would have walked ten miles to get a suit of armor, but now he'll spend ten sleepless nights making a new jacket instead. At one time, Claudio spoke plainly and to the point, but now he writes poetry and plays with words.

6. What does Benedick blame for the unfavorable changes he sees in Claudio?
   Benedick attributes the unfavorable changes to the fact that Claudio has fallen in love with Hero; Claudio is not the man he used to be.

7. What qualities must a woman possess before Benedick will even consider her for a wife?
   Benedick claims that she must be rich, wise, virtuous, fair, mild, noble, of good discourse, and an excellent musician.

8. What story do Don Pedro, Balthasar, and Claudio tell while Benedick is hiding in the arbor?
   Don Pedro, Balthasar, and Claudio talk about how much Beatrice is in love with Signior Benedick.

9. What knowledge do Don Pedro, Balthasar, and Claudio have that Benedick is not aware of?
   Don Pedro, Balthasar, and Claudio know that Benedick is in the arbor listening to every word. They want him to think that Beatrice loves him so that he will then fall in love with her.

10. What is Benedick's reaction to the news he overhears?
    He is stunned and changes his mind about never marrying. He claims that he will have Beatrice as his wife.

Act III, scenes i and ii:

1. What plan have Hero, Margaret, and Ursula agreed to participate in?
   The women know about Don Pedro's plans for Benedick, and they are going to do the same to Beatrice. They know that she is hiding nearby, so they begin a conversation in which they state that Benedick is on love with Beatrice.

2. Why does Hero claim that she will never tell Beatrice of Benedick's "affections?"
   As part of her ruse to get Beatrice to change her shrewish ways, Hero says that she would never tell Beatrice about Benedick's feelings because, since Beatrice is such a nasty person, she would make fun of poor Signior Benedick's affections toward her.

3. What is Beatrice's reaction to what she overhears?
   Beatrice feels badly for the way she has acted and she wants Benedick to "love on" because she is about to change her ways.

4. Where is Don Pedro headed after Claudio and Hero's wedding?
   He is planning to return home to Aragon. Claudio insists on accompanying him, but Don Pedro says that Claudio had better stay with his wife after the wedding.

5. What excuse does Benedick give for his melancholy behavior?
   Benedick claims to have a toothache.

6. What do Don Pedro and Claudio claim is "wrong" with Benedick?
    The men know that Benedick is pining for Beatrice.

7. What changes has Benedick made to his physical appearance?
    Benedick has shaved off his beard. It is possible that he overheard Beatrice's claim that she could not endure a man with a beard.

8. What false news does Don John bring to Don Pedro and Claudio?
    Don John claims that Hero is disloyal to Claudio with other men.

9. How does Don John intend to "prove" his accusations?
    Don John says that he, Don Pedro, and Claudio will stand below Hero's window that night to "witness" Hero's behavior. The reader is already aware that the woman at the window will be Margaret, not Hero.

10. What does Claudio intend to do if he finds out that Hero truly is inappropriately seeing other men?
    Claudio says that if what Don John says is true, then he will shame Hero publicly at the wedding.

Act III, scenes iii, iv, and v:

1. Who is Dogberry?
    Dogberry is the bumbling Constable of Messina.

2. What does the reader notice about Dogberry's and Verges's speeches?
    Both Dogberry and Verges use incorrect diction (malapropisms) when they speak. They confuse such words as "salvation" for "damnation" and "desertless" for "deserving." This adds to the comic relief of the play.

3. How does Dogberry instruct his watchmen to deal with any wrongdoers they may encounter?
    He tells the watchmen that they should speak to the offenders, but if the offenders do not comply with the watchmen's requests, the watchmen are to let them go on their way.

4. What do the watchmen happen to overhear?
    The watchmen overhear Borachio brag to Conrad about how he earned one thousand ducats from Don John for fooling Claudio into thinking that Hero was disloyal.

5. Describe Beatrice's mood during the scene with Hero and Margaret. To what does Hero contribute this mood?
    Beatrice is melancholy and claims that she is ill. Hero says that Beatrice is sick with love for Signior Benedick.

6. Describe the verbal banter among the women as they prepare for the wedding.
   The women, except Beatrice, are jovial and make many sexual puns as they prepare Hero for her wedding.

7. What does Dogberry tell Leonato right before the wedding and what is Leonato's reply?
   Dogberry insists that Leonato speak to him and cross-examine a pair of scoundrels that were arrested outside Leonato's house. Leonato says that he is too busy with his daughter's wedding and the Dogberry should just examine the offenders himself.

Act IV, scene i:

1. What is Claudio's response when the Friar asks if he comes to be married?
   He simply tells the Friar "no."

2. What does Claudio call Hero?
   He calls her a "rotten orange."

3. What is Claudio's accusation against Hero?
   Claudio claims that Hero is "an approved wanton" and that she has been unfaithful to him with Borachio. He tells those at the wedding that he saw Hero at the window with Borachio the night before.

4. How does Hero react to Count Claudio's claims?
   Hero first denies Claudio's accusations and then she faints.

5. Describe Leonato's reaction to the Count's accusations.
   Leonato believes the Count and denounces Hero as his daughter. He also wishes her dead.

6. Who defends Hero by saying that her blushes were from embarrassment and not from shame?
   The Friar defends Hero.

7. Who does Benedick suspect is behind the confusion surrounding Hero?
   Benedick believes that Don John is somehow involved in the confusion.

8. Describe the plan that the Friar creates regarding Hero.
   The Friar tells Leonato to publicly announce that Hero died after being accused, and that he should keep her hidden. The Friar believes that Claudio will feel remorse for his role in her "death" and eventually realize that he had been wrong about her faithfulness. If this does not work, the Friar says that Leonato can put Hero in a cloister.

9. What confession does Beatrice make to Benedick?
   Beatrice tells Benedick that she loves him.

10. What request does Beatrice make of Benedick?
    Beatrice demands that Benedick prove his love for her by killing Claudio for what he did to Hero.

Act IV, scene ii:

1. Of what crimes does Dogberry accuse Borachio and Conrad?
   Dogberry confuses his words and claims that Borachio and Conrad are accused of: perjury: for calling Don John a villain (confused with libel) and burglary: for accepting money for wrongly accusing Hero (confused with bribery).

2. What does Don John do after Hero is accused?
   Don John "secretly steals away" from Messina.

3. What does the Sexton suggest that Dogberry do with his prisoners?
   The Sexton suggests that Dogberry take them before Leonato and show him his examination of them.

4. For what "virtues" does Dogberry claim that he should be respected?
   Dogberry believes that he should be respected because he is wise, an officer of the law, and a landowner. He also claims that he is rich and handsome; therefore, he deserves respect.

Act V, scene i:

1. What advice does Antonio give his brother regarding his grief?
   Antonio tells Leonato to not take all the grief upon himself but to make those who caused the grief to suffer as well, namely Claudio and Don Pedro.

2. Why does Leonato challenge Claudio to a duel?
   Leonato challenges Claudio to a duel for wronging his innocent daughter.

3. How does Antonio defend Leonato?
   Antonio also challenges Claudio.

4. Why does Benedick also challenge Claudio?
   He challenges Claudio in response to Beatrice's request; to prove his love for Beatrice.

5. How does Don Pedro attempt to diffuse the situation between Claudio and Benedick?
   Don Pedro attempts to tease Benedick about Beatrice's behaviors; however, he does not realize that comments about Beatrice are no longer a joke to Benedick.

6. What news does Claudio learn from Borachio?
    When Dogberry brings the convicts forward, Borachio admits his part in the plot to disgrace Hero and that it was an unassuming Margaret at the window that night.

7. What does Claudio claim is his only sin in the events surrounding Hero's "death"?
    Claudio claims that his only sin in the whole situation is that he mistook Margaret for Hero.

8. What things does Leonato insist that Claudio do in order to restore his daughter Hero's honor?
    Claudio must: 1) publicly proclaim that he was wrong and Hero was innocent of any wrongdoing, 2) hang an epitaph on her tomb expressing her innocence, and 3) marry a "niece" of Leonato's that looks just like Hero.

Act V, scenes ii, iii, and iv:

1. Why does Beatrice want to know what happened between Benedick and Claudio?
    She hopes to hear that Benedick is planning to kill Claudio.

2. What does Claudio do at Hero's tomb?
    Claudio reads a poem that he wrote about Hero, and he hangs it on her tomb.

3. Who sings a hymn at Hero's tomb in her honor?
    Balthasar sings a hymn at Hero's tomb.

4. Who does Leonato claim were completely innocent in the accusations about Hero?
    Leonato claims that Hero, Claudio, and Don Pedro were innocent victims in Don John's plot.

5. Besides Don John, who does Leonato decide is also partly to blame for what happened to his daughter?
    Leonato claims that Margaret is also partly to blame for what happened to Hero.

6. What does Leonato instruct Hero, Margaret, Ursula, and Beatrice to do when Claudio arrives for the wedding ceremony?
    Leonato instructs the women to come in wearing masks.

7. How does Don Pedro describe Benedick's expression when he and Claudio enter?
    Don Pedro claims that Benedick has a "February face, so full of frost, or storm and cloudiness."

8. What does Claudio discover once the wedding party enters?
    Claudio learns that Hero is not really dead and that they are to be wed. All is forgiven.

9. What "evidence" do Claudio and Hero produce as proof that Benedick and Beatrice love each other?

> *Both Claudio and Hero produce sonnets that each has written about the other. Benedick and Beatrice then marry.*

STUDY GUIDE/QUIZ QUESTIONS - *Much Ado About Nothing*
Multiple Choice Format

Act I, scene i:
1. The messenger tells Leonato someone will be arriving in Messina. Who is coming?
    a. Don Juan from Spain
    b. Don Pedro of Aragon
    c. Count Claudio
    d. King Charles

2. Betrice questions the messenger about someone. Who?
    a. Don Pedro
    b. Signior Benedick
    c. Count Claudio
    d. Don John

3. According to Leonato, who is fighting a "merry war?"
    a. Don Pedro and Don John
    b. Count Claudio and Hero
    c. Leonato and Antonio
    d. Beatrice and Benedick

4. Describe Beatrice's greeting to Benedick upon his arrival.
    a. She immediately begins to insult him.
    b. She leaves the room because she cannot bear to look at him.
    c. She rushes into his arms and greets him with a kiss.
    d. She slaps his face for insulting her.

5. How long do Don Pedro and his company plan on staying in Messina?
    a. permanently
    b. a year
    c. a fortnight
    d. one month

6. Who is Don John?
    a. He is Don Pedro's long-lost brother who was recently found.
    b. He is Don Pedro's scheming brother who was recently taken back.
    c. He is a suitor for Beatrice who resents Signior Benedick's arrival.
    d. He is Signior Benedick's manservant.

7. Who catches Claudio's eye?
    a. Beatrice
    b. Margaret
    c. Hero
    d. Ursula

Much Ado About Nothing Multiple Choice Questions Act I, scene i page 2

8. What is it that Benedick swears will never happen to him?
   a. He swears that he will never be defeated in battle.
   b. He swears that he will never return to Messina after he leaves.
   c. He swears that he will never fall in love and marry.
   d. He swears that he will never allow himself to be insulted by a woman again.

9. Where does Claudio say he has spent time before coming to Messina?
   a. He has been traveling the world seeking the perfect bride.
   b. He has been at a university in a far away land.
   c. He has been at war.
   d. This is the first time he has ever left his home in Aragorn.

10. What does Don Pedro intend to do for Claudio?
    a. He intends to convince Beatrice to marry Claudio.
    b. He intends to woo Leonato's daughter Hero for the Count Claudio.
    c. He intends to make Claudio a knight of the realm.
    d. He intends to protect Claudio in all upcoming battles.

Act I, scenes ii and iii:

1. Who is Antonio?
    a. Claudio's father
    b. Benedick's manservant
    c. Don Pedro's brother
    d. Leonato's brother

2. What does Antonio claim to have learned from one of his servants?
    a. Antonio claims that Don Pedro intends to kill Claudio.
    b. Antonio claims that Benedick is in love with Beatrice.
    c. Antonio claims that Don Pedro intends to woo Leonato's daughter.
    d. Antonio claims that Hero has become engaged to Claudio.

3. What is Leonato's reaction to the news regarding Don Pedro's wooing his daughter?
    a. Leonato is delighted to hear this news.
    b. Leonato is outraged to hear this news.
    c. Leonato is surprised to hear this news.
    d. Leonato is never told that Don Pedro is wooing his daughter.

4. What are Don John's true feelings toward his brother, Don Pedro?
    a. Don John resents Don Pedro.
    b. Don John is angry that Don Pedro will not allow him to pursue Hero.
    c. Don John is happy to be reunited with Don Pedro after a long feud.
    d. Don John wants to kill his brother.

5. Who is Borachio?
    a. Don Pedro and Don John's youngest brother
    b. Hero's uncle
    c. Don John's companion
    d. Beatrice's suitor

6. What news does Borachio bring to Don John?
    a. Claudio and Hero are planning to elope.
    b. Don Pedro plans to woo Hero for Count Claudio.
    c. Benedick is plotting against Don Pedro.
    d. Leonato has given his permission for Hero to wed Claudio.

7. What does Don John plan to do regarding Claudio and Hero?
    a. Don John plans to arrange the wedding feast Claudio and Hero.
    b. Don John plans to discredit Claudio in Leonato's eyes.
    c. Don John plots to murder Claudio and marry Hero himself.
    d. Don John hopes to ruin Claudio's relationship with Don Pedro by foiling the plans surrounding Hero.

Act II, scene i:

1. Who does Leonato notice is not at supper that evening?
    a. Antonio
    b. Hero
    c. Claudio
    d. Don John

2. For what does Beatrice say she is thankful to God every night?
    a. her good health
    b. her chastity
    c. that she is not married
    d. her wit

3. Where does Beatrice say that, as an unmarried woman, she shall go?
    a. Beatrice will go to a convent.
    b. Beatrice will go to the gates of hell upon her death.
    c. Beatrice will go to heaven upon her death.
    d. Beatrice will go to an island for unmarried women.

4. What kind of party is Leonato hosting?
    a. Leonato is hosting an engagement party for Hero and Claudio.
    b. Lonato is hosting a birthday party for Beatrice.
    c. Leonato is hosting a welcome home party for Don Pedro.
    d. Leonato is hosting a masquerade party.

5. How does Beatrice further insult Benedick at Leonato's masquerade party?
    a. Beatrice, not knowing it is Benedick she is dancing with, talks negatively about him.
    b. Beatrice taunts him publicly at Leonato's party.
    c. Beatrice refuses Benedick's proposal of marriage in public.
    d. Beatrice tells Benedick that it is Hero who is in love with him, not her.

6. How does Don John feed false information to Claudio?
    a. Don John instructs Borachio to tell Claudio Don Pedro is wooing Hero.
    b. Don John leaves a note signed by Don Pedro.
    c. Don John tells Claudio when he is in a mask pretending to be Signior Benedick.
    d. Don John tells Claudio the truth, not lies about Don Pedro and Hero.

7. Who does Claudio become angry with after Don John shares what he has "heard?"
    a. Hero
    b. Don John
    c. Don Pedro
    d. Beatrice

Much Ado About Nothing Multiple Choice Questions Act II, scene i page 2

8. What hint does Beatrice drop about the possible reason for her treatment of Benedick?
    a. Benedick is a ladies man, and she doesn't trust him.
    b. Benedick lent his heart to her for a while, but he hurt her.
    c. Benedick is really in love with Hero and only pretends to like her.
    d. Beatrice thinks Benedick is a romantic fool.

9. What news does Don Pedro bring to Claudio?
    a. Don Pedro tells Claudio that Hero has refused to marry him.
    b. Don Pedro tells Claudio that he has won Hero's hand in marriage to Claudio.
    c. Don Pedro tells Claudio that Leonato has refused Claudio's suit.
    d. Don Pedro tells Claudio that Leonato has agreed to the match between Claudio and Hero.

10. What plan does Don Pedro begin to concoct?
    a. He plots to discredit Don John in Leonato's eyes.
    b. He plans the wedding feast for Claudio and Hero.
    c. He plots to bring Beatrice and Benedick together.
    d. He plans to kill Leonato and marry Hero.

Act II, scene ii and iii:

1. What plan does Borachio devise that pleases Don John?
    a. Borachio will use Margaret to discredit Hero in Claudio's eyes.
    b. Borachio will lure Don Pedro to a place where he can be easily ambushed.
    c. Borachio will foil Don Pedro's attempts to bring Benedick and Beatrice together.
    d. Borachio will woo Hero away from Claudio.

2. What does Don John promise Borachio if he is able to pull off his scheme?
    a. Don John promises him Hero's hand in marriage if he is successful.
    b. Don John promises him freedom from indentured servitude if he is successful.
    c. Don John promises him one thousand ducats if he is successful.
    d. Don John promises to promote him to commander if he is successful.

3. What information does Don John say he is going to obtain?
    a. Don John intends to learn the date of Beatrice and Benedick's wedding.
    b. Don John is going to obtain Claudio's battle plans.
    c. Don John is going to obtain enough evidence to have his brother jailed.
    d. Don John intends to learn the date of Claudio and Hero's wedding.

4. Why does Benedick send a servant to retrieve a book from his room?
    a. Benedick wants to be alone with his brooding about Claudio.
    b. Benedick needs the book to prove his love for Beatrice.
    c. Benedick wants to be alone to plot with Don John.
    d. It is the servant's job to serve Benedick in any way he sees fit.

5. Which of the following is not one of the changes in Claudio's behavior that Benedick notices?
    a. Claudio has begun to listen to chamber music.
    b. Claudio has shaved his beard.
    c. Claudio stays up late fashioning new clothes.
    d. Claudio has begun to speak and write in poetic form.

6. What does Benedick blame for the unfavorable changes he sees in Claudio?
    a. Claudio has fallen in love with Beatrice.
    b. Claudio has fallen in love with Hero.
    c. Claudio has contracted a terrible skin disease.
    d. Claudio has decided that the life of a soldier is entirely wrong.

7. For what reason must a woman posses specific qualities according to Benedick?
    a. She must posses these qualities in order to get to go to Heaven.
    b. She must posses these qualities to become a true lady.
    c. She must posses these qualities in order to represent her family properly.
    d. She must posses these qualities or he would never consider marrying her.

Much Ado About Nothing Multiple Choice Questions Act II, scene ii and iii page 2

8. What story do Don Pedro, Balthasar, and Claudio tell while Benedick is hiding in the arbor?
    a. They joke about how Don Pedro wooed Hero for Claudio.
    b. They plot the murder of Leonato.
    c. They talk about how Hero has been unfaithful to Claudio.
    d. They say that Beatrice is in love with Signior Benedick.

9. What knowledge do Don Pedro, Balthasar, and Claudio have that Benedick is not aware of?
    a. They know that Benedick is in the arbor listening.
    b. They know that Hero is truly in love with Benedick.
    c. They know that Don John plans to kill Benedick.
    d. They know that Leonato has planned to wed Beatrice and Benedick.

10. What is Benedick's reaction to the news he overhears?
    a. He is shocked that Hero is in love with him; he thinks she is too young.
    b. He is shocked that Beatrice loves him, and he says that he loves her as well.
    c. He is angry that Don John would plot against him.
    d. He is insulted that Leonato would assume that he would marry Beatrice.

Act III scene i and ii:

1. What plan have Hero, Margaret, and Ursula agreed to participate in?
    a. Don John's plot to discredit Don Pedro
    b. Don Pedro's plot to bring Beatrice and Benedick together
    c. Claudio's plan to elope with Hero
    d. Beatrice's plan to entice Benedick to be her husband

2. Why does Hero claim that she will never tell Beatrice of Benedick's "affections?"
    a. Beatrice would only make fun of Benedick's feelings.
    b. Beatrice wouldn't believe her anyway, so why bother?
    c. Beatrice is already in love with Don Pedro.
    d. Beatrice already knows that Benedick is in love with her.

3. What is Beatrice's reaction to what she overhears?
    a. She is angry at Benedick for mocking her.
    b. She feels bad for the way she has acted and wants Benedick to "love on" because she is about to change her ways.
    c. She is confused because she is already promised to Don Pedro, but she loves Benedick.
    d. She bursts into tears and says she can never face Benedick again.

4. Where is Don Pedro headed after Claudio and Hero's wedding?
    a. Rome
    b. Greece
    c. Messona
    d. Aragon

5. What excuse does Benedick give for his melancholy behavior?
    a. Claudio has forbid him to see Beatrice.
    b. He believes that Claudio is making a huge mistake in getting married to Hero.
    c. He is in love with Beatrice and does not know what to do.
    d. He claims to have a toothache.

6. What do Don Pedro and Claudio claim is "wrong" with Benedick?
    a. They know he is pining for Beatrice.
    b. He has eaten a "rotten orange."
    c. He misses his homeland.
    d. He is jealous of Claudio and Hero.

7. What change has Benedick made to his physical appearance?
    a. He has begun wearing nothing but black clothing.
    b. He has cut his hair and placed it in a locket for Beatrice.
    c. He has shaved off his beard.
    d. He has begun lifting heavy rocks to build muscles to impress Beatrice.

Much Ado About Nothing Multiple Choice Questions Act III, scenes i and ii page 2

8. What false news does Don John bring to Don Pedro and Claudio?
    a. He says that Leonato has suddenly taken ill.
    b. He says that Hero has run away with Conrad.
    c. He says that Hero is unfaithful to Claudio.
    d. He says that Hero has suddenly taken ill.

9. How does Don John intend to "prove" his accusations?
    a. He has a letter written by Hero to her lover.
    b. He, Don Pedro, and Claudio will hide below Hero's window and watch what happens.
    c. Beatrice has produced Hero's diary, and in it Hero writes of her visits from Borachio.
    d. He will threaten Hero upon pain of death to confess.

10. What does Claudio intend to do if he finds out that Hero truly is inappropriately seeing other men?
    a. Claudio intends to kill man who comes to see Hero.
    b. Claudio intends to kill Hero and her lover.
    c. Claudio intends to leave Messina immediately.
    d. Claudio intends to shame Hero publicly at the wedding.

Act III, scenes iii, iv, and v:

1. Who is Dogberry?
    a. the town constable
    b. Leonato's servant
    c. Beatrice's father
    d. Don John's accomplice

2. What does the reader notice about Dogberry's and Verges's speeches?
    a. They repeat each other constantly.
    b. They both us correct diction when they speak.
    c. They both use incorrect diction when they speak.
    d. Only Dogberry makes a speech.

3. How are the watchmen instructed to deal with any wrongdoers they may encounter?
    a. They are instructed to take them to Leonato for judgment.
    b. They are instructed to lock them in the town jail.
    c. They are instructed to speak to them; if they do not respond, let them go.
    d. They are instructed to tell the wrongdoers to correct their behavior.

4. What do the watchmen happen to overhear?
    a. They hear Borachio boast about earning one thousand ducats for discrediting Hero.
    b. They hear Borachio plotting to murder Leonato.
    c. They hear Dogberry plotting with Don John to convince Hero to leave Caludio.
    d. They hear Claudio's plan to publicly shame Hero at the wedding.

5. Describe Beatrice's mood during the scene with Hero and Margaret.
    a. Beatrice is happy and proclaims her love for Benedick.
    b. Beatrice is angry when Hero and Margaret make fun of her feelings for Benedick.
    c. Beatrice is quiet and claims to be tired.
    d. Beatrice is melancholy and claims that she is ill.

6. Describe the verbal banter among the women as they prepare for the wedding.
    a. The women make sexual puns as they prepare Hero for the wedding.
    b. The women try to convince Hero not to marry Claudio.
    c. The women tease Margaret when she admits her love for Borachio.
    d. The women tease Margaret about Borachio's late night visit.

7. Dogberry insists Leonato speak with him and cross-examine a pair of scoundrels who were arrested outside Leonato's house? What is Leonato's response?
    a. Leonato tells Dogberry to lock the them up, and he will deal with it later.
    b. Leonato tells Dogberry he is too busy with the wedding, take care of it himself.
    c. Leonato talks with the scoundrels and lets them go.
    d. Leonato talks with the scoundrels and knows the plan to discredit Hero.

Act IV, sceme i:

1. What is Claudio's response when the Friar asks if he comes to be married?
    a. He proclaims his undying love for Hero.
    b. He confesses his true love for Beatrice.
    c. He says "no."
    d. He refuses to speak at all; he is too angry.

2. What does Caludio call Hero?
    a. He calls her a "rotten orange."
    b. He calls her a fallen woman.
    c. He calls her the Devil's handmaiden.
    d. He calls her a "rotten mango."

3. What is Claudio's accusation against Hero?
    a. Claudio accuses her of being unfaithful to him with Borachio.
    b. Claudio accuses her of lying to her father about Beatrice and Benedick.
    c. Claudio accuses her of plotting with Don John to marry Benedick.
    d. Claudio accuses her of conspiring against him to win favor with Benedick.

4. How does Hero react to the Count's claims?
    a. She angrily storms out of the church.
    b. She denies the claims and then faints.
    c. She slaps Claudio for daring to speak to her in such a derogatory way.
    d. She cries and shamefully admits her guilt.

5. Describe Leonato's reaction to the Count's accusations.
    a. Leonato immediately challenges Claudio to a duel.
    b. Leonato takes his daughter away to protect her.
    c. Leonato attacks Claudio and has him locked in the dungeon.
    d. Leonato denounces Hero and wishes she were dead.

6. Who defends Hero by saying that her blushes were from embarrassment and not from shame?
    a. the Friar
    b. Benedick
    c. Beatrice
    d. Leonato

7. Who does Benedick suspect is behind the confusion surrounding Hero?
    a. Don Pedro
    b. Don John
    c. Beatrice
    d. Leonato

Much Ado About Nothing Multiple Choice Questions Act IV, scene i page 2

8. What plan does the Friar create regarding Hero?
    a. He plans to give her a potion that will make her appear to be dead, but she will really only be asleep.
    b. He tells Leonato to publicly announce that Hero died after being accused, and that he should keep her hidden. Then Claudio will feel remorse.
    c. He tells Leonato to put her away in a convent to avoid scandal.
    d. He plans to disguise Hero as a man so she can spy on Don John and expose him for the liar he is.

9. What confession does Beatrice make to Benedick?
    a. Beatrice confesses she was at the window with Borachio, not Hero.
    b. Beatrice confesses she is planning to leave Messina with Don John.
    c. Beatrice confesses she was involved in the plot against Hero.
    d. Beatrice confesses she loves Benedick.

10. What request does Beatrice make of Benedick?
    a. Beatrice demands Benedick kill Claudio to prove his love for her.
    b. Beatrice asks Benedick to run away with her.
    c. Beatrice asks Benedick to leave town immediately and to take Claudio with him.
    d. Beatrice demands Benedick proclaim his lover for her to Leonato.

Act IV, scene ii:

1. Of what crimes does Dogberry accuse Borachio and Conrad?
    a. He accuses them of defamation of character and theft.
    b. He accuses them of conspiracy and aiding a known felon.
    c. He accuses them of libel and bribery.
    d. He accuses them on perjury and burglary.

2. What does Don John do after Hero is accused?
    a. Claudio challenges him to a duel; Don John loses and leaves town.
    b. Benedick kills him when he finds out about the plot.
    c. He secretly leaves Messina.
    d. Don Pedro banishes him from Messina.

3. What does the Sexton suggest that Dogberry do with his prisoners?
    a. Dogberry should take them before Leonato to witness their cross-examination.
    b. Dogberry should lock them up for thirty days.
    c. Dogberry should publicly humiliate them.
    d. Dogberry should publicly execute them.

4. For what "virtues" does Dogberry claim that he should be respected?
    a. His fairness, his honesty, and his honor.
    b. His wisdom, his money, and his looks.
    c. His office, his judgement, and his personality.
    d. His open-mindedness, his integrity, and his smile.

Act V, scene i:

1. What advice does Antonio give his brother regarding his feelings?
    a. To forgive Hero and love her as his daughter
    b. To ask Claudio to leave Messina immediately for what he did to Hero
    c. To not take all the grief upon himself, but others should suffer as well
    d. To resist the urge to murder Don John

2. Why does Leonato challenge Claudio to a duel?
    a. Leonato challenges Claudio to a duel for planning to marry Beatrice not Hero.
    b. Leonato challenges Claudio to a duel for wronging his innocent daughter.
    c. Leonato challenges Claudio to a duel to prove he is the more powerful of the two.
    d. Leonato challenges Claudio to a duel because the Friar tells him it is the only way to save face.

3. How does Antonio defend Leonato?
    a. Antonio also challenges Claudio.
    b. Antonio kills Claudio after Claudio kills Leonato in the duel.
    c. Antonio discovers the plot and brings Don John to confront Claudio.
    d. Antonio does nothing to defend Leonato; he believes Claudio is right.

4. Why does Benedick also challenge Claudio?
    a. Benedick challenges Claudio to prove his loyalty to Leonato.
    b. Benedick does not challenge Claudio; he to believes Claudio is right.
    c. Benedick has always hated Claudio.
    d. Benedick challenges Claudio in response to Beatrice's request.

5. How does Don Pedro attempt to diffuse the situation surrounding Claudio and Benedick?
    a. He takes Claudio to the church to see Hero.
    b. He begins to tease Benedick about Beatrice, but does not realize comments about Beatrice are no longer a joke to Benedick.
    c. He agrees to help Claudio face Leonato's wrath.
    d. He tries to smooth things over between them by taking them to the local pub.

6. What news does Claudio learn from Borachio?
    a. Borachio tells Claudio that Hero never loved him.
    b. Borachio admits to that plot against Hero.
    c. Borachio announces that Don John has left town.
    d. Borachio tells Claudio that Leonato wants to fight him.

7. What does Claudio claim is his only sin in the events surrounding Hero's "death?"
    a. Claudio claims his only sin is how he humiliated Hero in public.
    b. Claudio claims his only sin was abandoning Hero at the altar.
    c. Claudio claims his only sin was mistaking Margaret for Hero.
    d. Claudio claims his only sin was causing Hero's death.

Much Ado About Nothing Multiple Choice Questions Act V, scene i page 2

8. Which of the following is **not** one of the things Leonato insists that Claudio do in order to restore his daughter Hero's honor?
    a. Claudio must sing a dirge at Hero's tomb in her memory.
    b. Claudio must hang an epitaph on Hero's tomb proclaiming her innocence.
    c. Claudio must publicly proclaim that he was wrong about Hero.
    d. Claudio must marry a niece who looks exactly like Hero in her place.

Act V, scenes ii, iii, and iv:

1. Why does Beatrice want to know what happened between Benedick and Claudio?
    a. She hopes to hear Claudio is leaving and never coming back.
    b. She hopes to hear that Benedick is planning to kill Claudio.
    c. She hopes they will resolve the problems and become great friends.
    d. She hopes Claudio will tell Benedick he loves Beatrice, not Hero.

2. What does Claudio do at Hero's tomb?
    a. Claudio sings a song of lament.
    b. Claudio places flowers on her grave and weeps openly.
    c. Claudio reads an epitaph he wrote to Hero.
    d. Claudio enters Hero's tomb to commit suicide, to be with her forever.

3. Who sings a hymn at Hero's tomb in her honor?
    a. Beatrice sings a hymn at Hero's tomb.
    b. Balthasar sings a hymn at Hero's tomb.
    c. The Friar sings a hymn at Hero's tomb.
    d. Margaret sings a hymn at Hero's tomb.

4. Who does Leonato claim were completely innocent in the accusations about Hero?
    a. He claims everyone played a part in the accusations against Hero.
    b. He claims Don Pedro is innocent.
    c. He claims Margaret and Benedick were innocent.
    d. He claims Hero, Claudio, and Don Pedro were all innocent.

5. Besides Don John, who does Leonato decide is also partly to blame for what happened to his daughter?
    a. Leonato claims that Margaret is also partly to blame.
    b. Leonato claims Hero is partly to blame.
    c. Leonato claims Dogberry is partly to blame.
    d. Leonato claims he is partly to blame.

6. What does Leonato instruct Hero, Margaret, Ursula, and Beatrice to do when Claudio arrives for the wedding ceremony?
    a. He instructs the women to come wearing masks.
    b. He instructs the women to refuse to speak to Claudio.
    c. He instructs the women to taunt Claudio as he enters the room.
    d. He instructs the women to greet Claudio warmly as he enters the room.

7. How does Don Pedro describe Benedick's expression when he and Claudio enter?
    a. "February, cold as stone, he will be alone."
    b. "February face, full of grace, never out of place."
    c. "February face, grey with the snow."
    d. "February face, so full of frost, or storm and cloudiness."

Much Ado About Nothing Multiple Choice Questions Act V, scene ii, iii, and iv page 2

8. What does Claudio discover once the wedding party enters?
    a. Hero is not really dead, and they are to be married immediately.
    b. He is being married to Margaret under Leonato's orders as a replacement for Hero.
    c. He was brought to the wedding so Benedick could kill him.
    d. All is forgiven and he is free to marry Beatrice.

9. What "evidence" do Claudio and Hero produce as proof that Benedick and Beatrice love each other?
    a. They produce the ring Benedick has for Beatrice.
    b. They produce a lock of Benedick's hair Beatrice has kept in a locket.
    c. They produce Beatrice's diary, in which she professes her love.
    d. They produce sonnets that each has written about the other.

ANSWER KEY - MULTIPLE CHOICE STUDY/QUIZ QUESTIONS - *Much Ado About Nothing*

	Act I, scene i	Act I, scenes ii and iii	Act II, scene i	Act II, scene ii and iii	Act III, scenes i and ii	Act III, scenes iii - v	Act IV, scene i	Act IV, scene ii	Act V, scene i	Act V, scenes ii - iv
1	B	D	D	A	B	A	C	C	C	B
2	B	C	C	C	A	C	A	C	B	C
3	D	A	B	D	B	C	A	A	A	B
4	A	A	D	A	D	A	B	B	D	D
5	D	C	A	B	D	D	D		B	A
6	B	B	C	B	A	A	A		B	A
7	C	D	A	D	C	B	B		C	D
8	C		B	D	C		B		A	A
9	C		B	A	B		D			D
10	B		C	B	D		A			

PRE-READING VOCABULARY WORKSHEETS

VOCABULARY Act I, scene i *Much Ado About Nothing*

Part I: Using Prior Knowledge and Contextual Clues

    Below are the sentences in which the vocabulary words appear in the text. Read the sentence. Use any clues you can find in the sentence combined with your prior knowledge, and write what you think the underlined words mean on the lines provided.

1. "He is very near by this. He was not three ***leagues*** off when I left him."

   _____

2. "You had musty ***victual***, and he hath holp to eat it. He is a very valiant trencherman: he hath an excellent stomach."

   _____

3. "You must not, sir, mistake my niece. There is a kind of merry war ***betwixt*** Signior Benedick and her."

   _____

4. "Is there no young ***squarer*** now that will make a voyage with him to the Devil?"

   _____

5. "O, Lord, he will hang upon him like a disease! He is sooner caught than the ***pestilence***, and the taker runs presently mad."

   _____

6. "...Courtesy itself must convert to disdain if you come into her presence."
   "Then is courtesy a ***turncoat***."

   _____

7. "They would else have been troubled with a ***pernicious*** suitor. I thank God and my cold blood, I am of your humor for that."

   _____

8. "...do you play the ***flouting*** Jack, to tell us Cupid is a good hare-finder and Vulcan a rare carpenter?"

   _____

Much Ado About Nothing Vocabulary Worksheet Act I, scene i Continued

9. "Thou wast ever an *obstinate* heretic in the despite of beauty."

_____

10. "My *liege*, your Highness now may do me good."

_____

Part II: Determining the Meaning
   Match the vocabulary words to their dictionary definitions

____ 1. league   A. feudal lord entitled to allegiance and service
____ 2. victuals   B. a unit of distance equal to 3.0 statute miles
____ 3. betwixt   C. a deadly or virulent epidemic disease
____ 4. squarer   D. causing harm or ruin
____ 5. pestilence   E. in the middle; between
____ 6. turncoat   F. firmly or stubbornly adhering to one's purpose or opinion
____ 7. pernicious   G. food supplies; provisions
____ 8. flouting   H. person who changes to an opposing idea or reverses principles
____ 9. obstinate   I. showing contempt for
____ 10. liege   J. a swashbuckler; one who delights in fighting

VOCABULARY Act I, scenes ii and iii *Much Ado About Nothing*

Part I: Using Prior Knowledge and Contextual Clues

Below are the sentences in which the vocabulary words appear in the text. Read the sentence. Use any clues you can find in the sentence combined with your prior knowledge, and write what you think the underlined words mean on the lines provided.

1. "The Prince and Count Claudio, walking in a thick-***pleached*** alley in mine orchard, were thus much overheard by a man of mine…"

   _____

2. "…the Prince discovered to Claudio that he loved my niece your daughter and meant to acknowledge it this night in a dance, and if he found her ***accordant,*** he meant to take the present time by the top and instantly break with you of it."

   _____

3. "…I will acquaint my daughter withal, that she may be the better prepared for an answer, if ***peradventure*** this be true."

   _____

4. "I wonder that thou…goest about to apply a moral medicine to a ***mortifying*** mischief."

   _____

5. "I had rather be a ***canker*** in a hedge than a rose in his grace…"

   _____

6. "…it better fits my blood to be ***disdained*** of all than to fashion a carriage to rob love from any."

   _____

7. "I am trusted with a muzzle and ***enfranchised*** with a clog; therefore, I have decreed not to sing in my cage."

   _____

8. "What is he for a fool who ***betroths*** himself to unquietness?"

   _____

Much Ado About Nothing Vocabulary Worksheet Act I, scenes ii and iii Continued

9. "Being entertained for a ***perfumer***, as I was smoking a musty room, comes me the Prince and Claudio, hand in hand in sad conference."

_____

10. "I whipt me behind the ***arras*** and there heard it agreed upon that the Prince should woo Hero for himself and, having obtained her, give her to Count Claudio."

_____

Part II: Determining the Meaning
    Match the vocabulary words to their dictionary definitions

    ____ 1. pleached   A. agreeable; compatible
    ____ 2. accordant   B. freed, as from bondage
    ____ 3. peradventure C. regarded or treated with haughty contempt; despised
    ____ 4. mortifying   D. humiliating or shameful, injurious to one's pride or self-respect
    ____ 5. canker   E. by chance; with doubt or uncertainty
    ____ 6. disdained   F. one who makes or sells perfumes
    ____ 7. enfranchised G. a fungal disease in plants or an ulcer in animals
    ____ 8. betroths   H. shaded or bordered with interlaced branches or vines
    ____ 9. perfumer   I. promises to give in marriage
    ____ 10. arras   J. a wall hanging, as a tapestry or similar object

VOCABULARY Act II, scene i *Much Ado About Nothing*

Part I: Using Prior Knowledge and Contextual Clues

Below are the sentences in which the vocabulary words appear in the text. Read the sentence. Use any clues you can find in the sentence combined with your prior knowledge, and write what you think the underlined words mean on the lines provided.

1. "How ***tartly*** that gentleman looks! I never can see him but I am heart-burned an hour after."

   _____

2. "By my troth, niece, thou wilt never get thee a husband if thou be so ***shrewd*** of thy tongue."

   _____

3. "…there will the Devil meet me like an old ***cuckold*** with horns on his head, and say, 'Get you to Heaven, Beatrice, get you to Heaven."

   _____

4. "Would it not grieve a woman to be over-mastered with a piece of valiant dust? To make an account of her life to a clod of wayward ***marl***?"

   _____

5. "For, hear me, Hero; wooing, wedding, and repenting is as a Scotch jig, a measure, and a ***cinquepace***…"

   _____

6. "Only his gift is in devising possible slanders. None but ***libertines*** delight in him; and the commendation is not in his wit but in his villainy…"

   _____

7. "I pray you, ***dissuade*** him from her; she is not equal for his birth."

   _____

8. "Alas, poor hurt fowl!! Now will he creep into ***sedges***."

   _____

9. "She speaks ***poniards***, and every word stabs."

   _____

53

Much Ado About Nothing Vocabulary Worksheet Act II, scene i Continued

10. "…while she is here, a man may live as quiet in hell as in a sanctuary, and people sin upon purpose, because they would go thither; so indeed all disquiet, horror, and ***perturbation*** follows her."

_____

Part II: Determining the Meaning
    Match the vocabulary words to their dictionary definitions

    ___ 1. tartly   A. those who act without moral restraint
    ___ 2. shrewd   B. earthy mix of clay used as a fertilizer
    ___ 3. cuckold   C. mental disquiet, disturbance, or agitation
    ___ 4. marl   D. sharp in character, spirit, or expression; cutting
    ___ 5. cinquepace   E. lively dance, the steps of which were regulated by the number five
    ___ 6. libertines   F. sharp or ill-tempered
    ___ 7. dissuade   G. to advise or urge against
    ___ 8. sedges   H. daggers typically having slender square or triangular blades
    ___ 9. poniards   I. grass-like plants having solid stems, leaves in three vertical rows
    ___ 10. perturbation J. the husband of an unfaithful wife

VOCABULARY Act II, scenes ii and iii *Much Ado About Nothing*

Part I: Using Prior Knowledge and Contextual Clues

Below are the sentences in which the vocabulary words appear in the text. Read the sentence. Use any clues you can find in the sentence combined with your prior knowledge, and write what you think the underlined words mean on the lines provided.

1. "Any bar, any cross, any *impediment* will be medicinable to me."

   _____

2. "Not honestly, my lord, but so *covertly* that no dishonesty shall appear in me."

   _____

3. "…intend a kind of zeal both to the Prince and Claudio, as—in love of your brother's honor, who hath made this match, and his friend's reputation, who is thus like to be *cozened* with the semblance of a maid—that you have discovered thus."

   _____

4. "I do wonder that one man, seeing how much another man is a fool when he dedicates his behaviors to love, will, after he hath laughed at such shallow *follies* in others, becomes the argument of his own scorn by falling in love."

   _____

5. "I have known when there was no music with him but the drum and the fife; and now had he rather hear the *tabor* and the pipe."

   _____

6. "He was wont to speak plain and to the purpose, like an honest man and a soldier; and now is he turned *orthography*: his words are a very fantastical banquet—just so many strange dishes."

   _____

7. "No, nor I neither; but most wonderful that she should so *dote* on Signior Benedick, whom she hath in all outward behaviors seemed ever to abhor."

   _____

8. "It seems her affections have their full bent. Love me? Why, it must be *requited*. I hear how I am censured."

   _____

Much Ado About Nothing Vocabulary Worksheet Act II, scenes ii and iii Continued

9. "They say the lady is fair—'tis a truth, I can bear them witness; and virtuous—'tis so, I cannot **reprove** it…"

_____

10. "You take pleasure then in the message?"
 "Yea, just so much as you may take upon a knife's point and choke a ***daw*** withal."

_____

Part II: Determining the Meaning
  Match the vocabulary words to their dictionary definitions

  ____ 1. impediment   A. to bestow or express excessive love or fondness habitually
  ____ 2. covertly   B. simpleton; fool
  ____ 3. cozened   C. small drum
  ____ 4. follies   D. in a concealed, secret, or disguised manner
  ____ 5. tabor   E. to make a payment or return for
  ____ 6. orthography   F. obstruction; hindrance; obstacle
  ____ 7. dote   G. the art of writing
  ____ 8. requited   H. misled by means of a petty trick or fraud; deceived
  ____ 9. daw   I. acts lacking of good sense, understanding, or foresight
  ____ 10. reprove   J. to criticize or correct

VOCABULARY Act III, scenes i and ii *Much Ado About Nothing*

Part I: Using Prior Knowledge and Contextual Clues

Below are the sentences in which the vocabulary words appear in the text. Read the sentence. Use any clues you can find in the sentence combined with your prior knowledge, and write what you think the underlined words mean on the lines provided.

1. "The pleasantest ***angling*** is to see the fish cut with her golden oars the silver stream and greedily devour the treacherous bait."

   _____

2. "I know her spirits are as coy and wild as ***haggards*** of the rock."

   _____

3. "I never yet saw man, how wise, how noble, young, how rarely featured, but she would spell him backward. If fair-faced, she would swear the gentleman should be her sister... If low, an ***agate*** very vilely cut..., so turns she every man the wrong side out..."

   _____

4. "Sure, sure, such ***carping*** is not commendable."

   _____

5. "If thou dost love, my kindness shall ***incite*** thee to bind our loves in a holy band..."

   _____

6. "I'll bring you thither, my lord, if you'll ***vouchsafe*** me."

   _____

7. "You may think that I love you not. Let that appear hereafter, and aim better at me by that I now will ***manifest***."

   _____

8. "...I think he holds you well and in dearness of heart hath holp to effect your ***ensuing*** marriage—surely suit ill spent and labor ill bestowed!"

   _____

Much Ado About Nothing Vocabulary Worksheet Act III, scenes i and ii Continued

9. "I will ***disparage*** her no farther till you are my witnesses. Bear it coldly but till midnight and let the issue show itself."

_____

10. "O mischief strangely ***thwarting***!"

_____

Part II: Determining the Meaning
    Match the vocabulary words to their dictionary definitions

    ___ 1. angling   A. to stir, encourage, or urge on; stimulate or prompt to action
    ___ 2. haggards   B. petty faultfinding
    ___ 3. agate   C. to make clear or evident to the eye or the understanding
    ___ 4. carping   D. to allow or permit, as by favor or graciousness
    ___ 5. incite   E. opposing and defeating the efforts, plans, or ambitions of
    ___ 6. vouchsafe   F. to speak of or treat slightingly; depreciate; belittle
    ___ 7. manifest   G. a type of stone showing curved, colored bands or other markings
    ___ 8. ensuing   H. finshing with hook and line
    ___ 9. disparage   I. following as a consequence or result
    ___ 10. thwarting   J. adult hawks captured for training

VOCABULARY Act III, scenes iii through v *Much Ado About Nothing*

Part I: Using Prior Knowledge and Contextual Clues

Below are the sentences in which the vocabulary words appear in the text. Read the sentence. Use any clues you can find in the sentence combined with your prior knowledge, and write what you think the underlined words mean on the lines provided.

1. "Why then, take no note of him but let him go, and presently call the rest of the watch together and thank God you are rid of a ***knave***."

_____

2. "If we know him to be a thief, shall we not lay hands on him?"
   "Truly, by your office, you may; but I think that they that touch pitch will be ***defiled***."

_____

3. "This is the end of the charge: you, ***constable***, are to present the Prince's own person."

_____

4. "Thou knowest that the fashion of a ***doublet***, or a hat, or a cloak, is nothing to a man."

_____

5. "Seest thou not, I say, what a deformed thief this fashion is? How giddily 'a turns about all the hot-bloods between fourteen and five-and-thirty? Sometimes fashioning them…like the shaven Hercules in the smirched, worm-eaten tapestry, where his ***codpiece*** seems as massy as his club?"

_____

6. "We here have recovered the most dangerous piece of ***lechery*** that ever was known in the commonwealth."

_____

7. "We are like to prove a goodly ***commodity***, being taken up of these men's bills."

_____

8. Get you some of this distilled Carduus benedictus and lay it to your heart. It is the only thing for a ***qualm***."

_____

Much Ado About Nothing Vocabulary Worksheet Act III, scenes iii through v Continued

9. "The Prince, the Count, Signior Benedick, Don John, and all the **gallants** of the town are come to fetch you to church."

_____

10. "Comparisons are odorous. Palabras, neighbor Verges."
    "Neighbors, you are **tedious**."

_____

Part II: Determining the Meaning
   Match the vocabulary words to their dictionary definitions

   ___ 1. knave   A. a sudden feeling of apprehensive uneasiness
   ___ 2. defiled   B. an officer of the peace, having police and minor judicial functions
   ___ 3. constable   C. a cover for the crotch in men's hose or tight-fitting breeches
   ___ 4. doublet   D. made filthy or dirty; unclean
   ___ 5. codpiece   E. boring, tiring, monotonous, dull
   ___ 6. lechery   F. fashionable young men
   ___ 7. commodity   G. a close-fitting outer garment worn by men in the Renaissance
   ___ 8. qualm   H. an article of trade or commerce
   ___ 9. gallants   I. an unprincipled, untrustworthy, or dishonest person
   ___ 10. tedious   J. unrestrained or excessive indulgence of sexual desire

VOCABULARY Act IV, scene i *Much Ado About Nothing*

Part I: Using Prior Knowledge and Contextual Clues

Below are the sentences in which the vocabulary words appear in the text. Read the sentence. Use any clues you can find in the sentence combined with your prior knowledge, and write what you think the underlined words mean on the lines provided.

1. "Give not this rotten orange to your friend: she's but the sign and **semblance** of her honor."

   _____

2. "[I mean] Not to be married, not to knit my soul to an approved **wanton**."

   _____

3. "O, God defend me! How I am beset! What kind of **catechizing** call you this?"

   _____

4. "…let her awhile be secretly kept in and publish it that she is dead indeed; maintain a mourning **ostentation**, and on your family's old monument hang mournful epitaphs…"

   _____

5. "But not for that dream I on this strange course, but for this **travail** look for greater birth."

   _____

6. "Thou seest that all the grace that she hath left is that she will not add to her damnation a sin of **perjury**: she not denies it."

   _____

7. "Time hath not yet so dried this blood of mine, nor age so eat up my invention, nor fortune made such **havoc** of my means…to quit me of them thoroughly."

   _____

8. "…on your family's old monument, hang mournful epitaphs and do all rites that **appertain** unto a burial."

   _____

Much Ado About Nothing Vocabulary Worksheet Act IV, scene i Continued

9. "But if all aim but this be leveled false, the supposition of the lady's death will quench the wonder of her *infamy*."

_____

10. "By this hand, Claudio shall *render* me a dear account."

_____

Part II: Determining the Meaning
    Match the vocabulary words to their dictionary definitions

    ____ 1. semblance   A. painfully difficult or burdensome work; toil
    ____ 2. wanton   B. the willful giving of false testimony under oath
    ____ 3. catechizing   C. great destruction or devastation; ruinous damage
    ____ 4. ostentation   D. outward aspect or appearance
    ____ 5. travail   E. extremely bad reputation
    ____ 6. perjury   F. conspicuous show or display intended to impress others
    ____ 7. havoc   G. sexually lawless or unrestrained
    ____ 8. appertain   H. instruction by means of question and answer
    ____ 9. infamy   I. provide; submit for inspection
    ____ 10. render   J. to belong as a part, right, possession, attribute

VOCABULARY Act IV, scene ii *Much Ado About Nothing*

Part I: Using Prior Knowledge and Contextual Clues

Below are the sentences in which the vocabulary words appear in the text. Read the sentence. Use any clues you can find in the sentence combined with your prior knowledge, and write what you think the underlined words mean on the lines provided.

1. "O, a stool and a cushion for the **sexton**."

___

2. "Which be the **malefactors**? ... [Which} are the offenders that are to be examined?"

___

3. "Come you **hither**, sirrah. A word in your ear."

___

4. "O villain! Thou wilt be condemned into everlasting **redemption** for this."

___

5, 6. Dogberry: Come, let them be opinioned.
Verges: Let them be in the hands –
Conrad: Off, **coxcomb**!
Dogberry: God's my life, where's the sexton? Let him write down the prince's officer **coxcomb**. Come, bind them. – Thou naughty **varlet**!

___

7. "No, thou villain, thou art full of **piety**, as shall be proved upon thee by good witness."

___

Much Ado About Nothing Vocabulary Worksheet Act IV, scene ii Continued

Part II: Determining the Meaning
Match the vocabulary words to their dictionary definitions

___ 1. malefactors   A. a person employed to take care of a church
___ 2. sexton   B. being saved from error or evil
___ 3. hither   C. the quality of being devoutly religious
___ 4. redemption   D. to or toward this place
___ 5. coxcomb   E. a rascal; a knave
___ 6. varlet   F. those who have committed a crime; criminals
___ 7. piety   G. a vain and often foolish person

VOCABULARY Act V, scene i *Much Ado About Nothing*

Part I: Using Prior Knowledge and Contextual Clues

Below are the sentences in which the vocabulary words appear in the text. Read the sentence. Use any clues you can find in the sentence combined with your prior knowledge, and write what you think the underlined words mean on the lines provided.

1. "I pray thee cease thy counsel, which falls into mine ears as profitless as water in a ***sieve***."

   _____

2. "…but tasting it, their counsel turns to passion, which before would give ***preceptial*** medicine to rage, fetter strong madness in a silken thread, charm ache with air and agony with words."

   _____

3. "Marry, thou does wrong me, thou ***dissembler***, thou!"

   _____

4. "God knows I loved my niece, and she is dead, ***slandered*** to death by villains that dare as well answer a man indeed as I dare take a serpent by the tongue."

   _____

5. "I know them, yea, and what they weigh, even to the utmost ***scruple***, scambling, outfacing, fashion-monging boys, that lie and cog, and flout, deprave and slander…and speak off half a dozen dang'rous words, how they might hurt their enemies, if they durst…"

   _____

6. "You are almost come to part almost a ***fray***."
   "We had like to have had our noses snapped off with two old men without teeth."

   _____

7. "In a false quarrel there is no true ***valor***."

   _____

8. "We have been up and down to seek thee; for we are high-proof ***melancholy*** and would fain have it beaten away."

   _____

Much Ado About Nothing Vocabulary Worksheet Act V, scene I Continued

9. "I' faith, I thank him, he hath bid me to a calve's head and a ***capon***, the which if I do not carve most curiously, say my knife's naught."

_____

10. "***Hearken*** after their offense, my lord."

_____

Part II: Determining the Meaning
    Match the vocabulary words to their dictionary definitions

    ___ 1. sieve   A. a procedural directive or rule
    ___ 2. preceptial   B. made false and malicious statements or reports about someone
    ___ 3. dissembler   C. a noisy fight
    ___ 4. slandered   D. a gloomy state of mind, depressed
    ___ 5. scruple   E. to give heed or attention to what is said; listen
    ___ 6. fray   F. a castrated male chicken
    ___ 7. valor   G. boldness or determination in facing great danger
    ___ 8. melancholy   H. a very small portion or amount
    ___ 9. capon   I. one who gives a false or misleading appearance
    ___ 10. hearken   J. a perforated utensil used for straining or sifting

VOCABULARY Act V, scenes ii through iv *Much Ado About Nothing*

Part I: Using Prior Knowledge and Contextual Clues

Below are the sentences in which the vocabulary words appear in the text. Read the sentence. Use any clues you can find in the sentence combined with your prior knowledge, and write what you think the underlined words mean on the lines provided.

1. "Thy wit is as quick as the greyhound's mouth; it catches."
   "And yours as blunt as the fencer's *foils*, which hit but hurt not."

   _____

2. "I can find no rhyme to 'lady' but 'baby'—an innocent rhyme; for 'scorn,' 'horn'—a hard rhyme; for 'school,' 'fool'—a babbling rhyme: very *ominous* endings!"

   _____

3. "For them all together, which maintained so politic a state of evil that they will not admit any good part to *intermingle* with them."

   _____

4. "Suffer love!—a good *epithet*! I do suffer love indeed, for I love thee against my will."

   _____

5. "If a man do not erect in this age his own tomb ere he dies, he shall live no longer in monument than the bell rings and the widow weeps."
   "And how long is that, think you?"
   "Question: why an hour in *clamor* and a quarter in rheum."

   _____

6. "Therefore is it most *expedient* for the wise, if Don Worm find no impediment to the contrary, to be the trumpet of his own virtues, as I am to myself."

   _____

7. "Well, I am glad that all things sort so well."
   "And so am I, being else by faith enforced to call young Claudio to a *reckoning* for it."

   _____

8. "Your answer, sir, is *enigmatical*."

   _____

Much Ado About Nothing Vocabulary Worksheet Act V, scenes ii through iv Continued

9. "I had well hoped thou wouldst have denied Beatrice, that I might have *cudgeled* thee out of thy single life, to make thee a double-dealer…"

___

Part II: Determining the Meaning
    Match the vocabulary words to their dictionary definitions

  ___ 1. foils   A. fencing swords having a circular guard and thin, flexible blades
  ___ 2. ominous   B. struck or beat with a stick
  ___ 3. intermingle   C. portending evil or harm; foreboding; threatening
  ___ 4. epithet   D. perplexing; mysterious
  ___ 5. clamor   E. to mix or become mixed together
  ___ 6. expedient   F. fit or suitable for the purpose; proper under the circumstances
  ___ 7. cudgeled   G. the settlement of accounts or of a score
  ___ 8. reckoning   H. a loud uproar, as from a crowd of people
  ___ 9. enigmatical   I. any word or phrase applied to a person to describe an actual or attributed quality

VOCABULARY ANSWER KEY- *Much Ado About Nothing*

	Act I, scene i	Act I, scenes ii and iii	Act II, scene i	Act II, scene ii and iii	Act III, scenes i and ii	Act III, scenes iii - v	Act IV, scene i	Act IV, scene ii	Act V, scene i	Act V, scenes ii - iv
1	B	H	D	F	H	I	D	F	J	A
2	G	A	F	D	J	D	G	A	A	C
3	E	E	J	H	G	B	H	D	I	E
4	J	D	B	I	B	G	F	B	B	I
5	C	G	E	C	A	C	A	G	H	H
6	H	C	A	G	D	J	B	E	C	F
7	D	B	G	A	C	H	C	C	G	B
8	I	I	I	E	I	A	J		D	G
9	F	F	H	B	F	F	E		F	D
10	A	J	C	J	E	E	I		E	

DAILY LESSONS

LESSON ONE

Objectives
1. To become familiar with William Shakespeare, the author of *Much Ado About Nothing*
2. To become familiar with elements of Shakespearean Language, specifically blank verse
3. To introduce the *Much Ado About Nothing* play
4. To distribute books, study questions, and other related materials
5. To preview the vocabulary worksheet and study guide questions for Act I, scene i
6. To read Act I, scene i

Activity #1
Ask students to brainstorm all they have heard of regarding William Shakespeare and share their ideas aloud. Someone in the class will probably come up with "Shakespeare is hard... he doesn't write in English!" That will lead into the discussion of Shakespeare's language.

Ask students to brainstorm any poems or songs that they know by heart. Students share ideas aloud and write them on the chalk board. Then ask them what made it easy/difficult to memorize the pieces. (Hopefully they will mention a "beat" or a rhyme scheme...if not, lead them that way). This will lead into the discussion of meter in English poetry and Shakespeare's use of blank verse for many of his characters' lines. The use of blank verse (unrhymed iambic pentameter) made the lines easier for the actor to memorize, especially in a short period of time. (See exercises below about meter and blank verse: worksheet included)

Activity #2
Break the class into seven groups and distribute Blank Verse worksheets. Assign each group one of the passages from the worksheet and have the students break the speech into its poetic lines. Encourage them to bang on their desks as they do so!

Activity #3
Distribute the materials students will use in this unit. Explain in detail how students are to use these materials.

Study Guides Students should read the study guide questions for each reading assignment prior to beginning the reading assignment to get a feeling for what events and ideas are important in the section they are about to read. After reading the section, students will (as a class or individually) answer the questions to review the important events and ideas from that section of the play. Students should keep the study guides as study materials for the unit test.

Vocabulary Prior to each reading assignment, students will do vocabulary work related to the section of the book they are about to read. Following the completion of the reading of the play, there will be a vocabulary review of all the words used in the vocabulary assignments. Students should keep their vocabulary work as study materials for the unit test.

Reading Assignment Sheet You need to fill in the reading assignment sheet to let students know by when their reading has to be completed. You can either write the assignment sheet up on a side blackboard or bulletin board and leave it there for students to see each day, or you can photocopy schedules for each student to have. In either case, you should advise students to become very familiar with the reading assignments so they know what is expected of them.

<u>Extra Activities Center</u> The Unit Resource Materials portion of this LitPlan contains suggestions for an extra library of related books and articles in your classroom as well as crossword and word search puzzles. Make an extra activities center in your room where you will keep these materials for students to use. (Bring the books and articles in from the library and keep several copies of the puzzles on hand.) Explain to students that these materials are available for students to use when they finish reading assignments or other class work early.

<u>Nonfiction Assignment Sheet</u> Explain to students that they each are to read at least one non-fiction piece from the in-class library at some time during the unit. Students will fill out a nonfiction assignment sheet after completing the reading to help you (the teacher) evaluate their reading experiences and to help the students think about and evaluate their own reading experiences.

<u>Books</u> Each school has its own rules and regulations regarding student use of school books. Advise students of the procedures that are normal for your school. Preview the book. Look at the covers, front-matter, and index. Glance through at some of the drawings.

Activity #4

Have students look at and read through the study questions for Act I, scene i. This can be done silently or orally.

Activity #5

Do the first vocabulary worksheet (for Act I, scene i) orally, together as a class, to show students how the vocabulary worksheets should be done prior to each reading assignment.

Activity #6

Assign roles for Act I of *Much Ado About Nothing* to students. Those students, when doing their homework, should prepare to read the parts aloud in class in lesson 3. Encourage them to PERFORM, not just read the words.

All students should read Act I, scene i prior to the next class period. If time remains in class, students may begin reading silently.

Meter in English Poetry: the metrical foot

The word "meter" comes from the Greek word for "measure." The term refers to a pattern of stressed and unstressed **syllables** (NOT words) in a poetic line. In English poetry, meter is determined by the number of **stresses** per line, and usually a poem written in metrical verse will keep to a basic, identifiable pattern, though variation may be achieved through deliberate substitution of different metrical feet into the basic pattern. In musical terms (for those of you who read music), just as the number of beats per measure will determine the time signature, the number of stresses per line will determine a poem's meter. As in music, eighth or sixteenth notes are commonly used to add variety without changing the song's time signature, so are variations in the metrical foot occasionally used to vary the sound of a particular line without changing the poem's overall meter.

The conventional symbols used in scansion are "/", to indicate a **stressed syllable** (think of a drum stick beating time), and "U", to indicated an **unstressed syllable** (think of a smiley face for "unstressed").

The **metrical foot** is the basic unit of meter. The most common metrical feet and their patterns of stressed and unstressed syllables are as follows:

iamb:	U /	Dani**elle**
trochee:	/ U	**Su**san
anapest:	U U /	Desi**ree**
dactyl:	/ U U	**Chris**topher

The meter of a poem is determined by the predominant metrical foot, and by the number of feet per line that predominates in the poem. The following terms indicate the number of feet per line:

monometer:	one **foot** per line
dimeter:	two **feet** per line
trimeter:	three **feet** per line
tetrameter:	four **feet** per line
pentameter:	five **feet** per line
hexameter:	six **feet** per line
heptameter:	seven **feet** per line
octameter:	eight **feet** per line

This is how the terms are used to describe the meter of a poem (the suffix "-ic" means "made of"):

A poem written in predominantly **iambic** meter, with **five feet** per line, would be called "**iambic pentameter**." One written in primarily **trochaic** meter, with **four feet** per line, would be "**trochaic tetrameter**." One written in **anapestic** meter, with three feet per line, would be "**anapestic trimeter**."

Now that you understand the concept of meter in poetry, let's talk about how this fits into our study of Shakespeare.

William Shakespeare wrote most of the dialogue for his plays in what is known as **blank verse,** or unrhymed iambic pentameter. This means that each line has ten **syllables (not necessarily ten words)**, and every even (2nd, 4th, 6th, 8th, and 10th) syllable was stressed. Examine the following from Shakespeare's *Romeo and Juliet*:

O, **then**, I **see** Queen **Mab** hath **been** with **you**.
She **is** the **fair**ies' **mid**wife, **and** she **comes**
In **shape** no **big**ger **than** an **a**gate-**stone**
On **the** fore-**fin**ger **of** an **al**der**man**,
Drawn **with** a **team** of **lit**tle **a**tom**ies**
A**thwart** men's **no**ses **as** they **lie** a**sleep**;

Note that every even syllable has been bolded; these are what get the vocal stress when read aloud. Try reading the lines slowly and beat your hand on the desk for each of the stressed syllables… what do you hear? You should be able to distinguish a repetitive vocal pattern that is easy to remember. Read the lines a few times and then try them with your eyes closed. You will be surprised at how much you will already be able to remember! Note that in this passage, none of the lines rhyme. This pattern of five beats per line and having no rhyme scheme is an example of blank verse.

Sometimes, though, it is necessary to run two syllables together quickly in order to fit the correct words into the pattern. Keep in mind that even though there may not be PERFECT stressed, unstressed syllables, the overall meter is still iambic pentameter. For example, when you listen to a song that is written in 4:4 time, every quarter note gets the beat, and there are 4 beats per measure. Well, sometimes a musician needs to add an extra note, and so he replaces one of the quarter notes with two eighth notes instead. Even though the beat is briefly altered, the song is still written in 4:4 time.

Consider the following from *Romeo and Juliet*:

But **soft**, what **light** through **yon**der **win**dow **breaks**?
It **is** the **East**, and **Ju**liet **is** the **sun**.
A**rise**, fair **Sun**, and **kill** the **en**vious **Moon**
That **is** already **sick** and **pale** with **grief**
That **thou**, her **maid**, art **far** more **fair** than **she**.

Notice that the word "Juliet" (which is three syllables) emphasizes only the first syllable. The second two are rushed through (like two eighth notes) to make the next beat on "time". The same is true for the word "envious".

Ok, now that you are a blank verse expert, let's try to put these speeches from *Much Ado About Nothing* into their proper lines. It's okay to bang on your desk as you work out the meter!

Shakespeare's Language: Blank Verse

Blank verse is defined as unrhymed iambic pentameter. Examine each of the following speeches made by characters in *Much Ado About Nothing*. The lines have been broken and have been written as prose. Using what you have learned about blank verse, break the paragraphs into their proper lines.

1. Thou wilt be like a lover presently and tire the hearer with a book of words. If thou dost love fair Hero, cherish it, and I will break with her and with her father, and thou shalt have her. Was't not to this end that thou began'st to twist so fine a story?

2. What need the bridge much broader than the flood? The fairest grant is the necessity. Look, what will serve is fit: 'tis once, thou lovest, and I will fit thee with the remedy. I know we shall have reveling to-night: I will assume thy part in some disguise and tell fair Hero I am Claudio.

3. And in her bosom I'll unclasp my heart and take her hearing prisoner with the force and strong encounter of my amorous tale: then after to her father will I break; and the conclusion is, she shall be thine. In practice let us put it presently.

4. Now, Ursula, when Beatrice doth come, as we do trace this alley up and down, our talk must only be of Benedick. When I do name him, let it be thy part to praise him more than ever man did merit.

5. Sweet prince, you learn me noble thankfulness. There, Leonato, take her back again: give not this rotten orange to your friend; she's but the sign and semblance of her honour. Behold how like a maid she blushes here! O, what authority and show of truth can cunning sin cover itself withal!

6. O Hero, what a Hero hadst thou been, if half thy outward graces had been placed about thy thoughts and counsels of thy heart! But fare thee well, most foul, most fair! farewell, thou pure impiety and impious purity!

7. Wherefore! Why, doth not every earthly thing cry shame upon her? Could she here deny the story that is printed in her blood? Do not live, Hero; do not ope thine eyes: for, did I think thou wouldst not quickly die, thought I thy spirits were stronger than thy shames, myself would, on the rearward of reproaches, strike at thy life. Grieved I, I had but one? Chid I for that at frugal nature's frame? O, one too much by thee! Why had I one?

Shakespeare's Language: Blank Verse Answers

ANSWERS (lines returned to blank verse):

1. Don Pedro:

Thou wilt be like a lover presently
And tire the hearer with a book of words.
If thou dost love fair Hero, cherish it,
And I will break with her and with her father,
And thou shalt have her. Was't not to this end
That thou began'st to twist so fine a story?

2. Don Pedro:

What need the bridge much broader than the flood?
The fairest grant is the necessity.
Look, what will serve is fit: 'tis once, thou lovest,
And I will fit thee with the remedy.
I know we shall have revelling to-night:
I will assume thy part in some disguise
And tell fair Hero I am Claudio

3. Don Pedro:

And in her bosom I'll unclasp my heart
And take her hearing prisoner with the force
And strong encounter of my amorous tale:
Then after to her father will I break;
And the conclusion is, she shall be thine.
In practise let us put it presently.

4. Hero:

Now, Ursula, when Beatrice doth come,
As we do trace this alley up and down,
Our talk must only be of Benedick.
When I do name him, let it be thy part
To praise him more than ever man did merit

5. Claudio:

Sweet prince, you learn me noble thankfulness.
There, Leonato, take her back again:
Give not this rotten orange to your friend;
She's but the sign and semblance of her honour.
Behold how like a maid she blushes here!
O, what authority and show of truth
Can cunning sin cover itself withal!

6. Claudio:

O Hero, what a Hero hadst thou been,
If half thy outward graces had been placed
About thy thoughts and counsels of thy heart!
But fare thee well, most foul, most fair! farewell,
Thou pure impiety and impious purity!

7. Leonato:

Wherefore! Why, doth not every earthly thing
Cry shame upon her? Could she here deny
The story that is printed in her blood?
Do not live, Hero; do not ope thine eyes:
For, did I think thou wouldst not quickly die,
Thought I thy spirits were stronger than thy shames,
Myself would, on the rearward of reproaches,
Strike at thy life. Grieved I, I had but one?
Chid I for that at frugal nature's frame?
O, one too much by thee! Why had I one?

LESSON TWO

Objectives
1. To review the main events and ideas from Act I, scene i
2. To distribute the non-fiction assignment about Shakespeare and Elizabethan Theatre
3. To enhance research skills through a visit to the school's library/media center
4. To demonstrate reading comprehension skills through completion of a non-fiction worksheet
5. To preview the study guide questions and vocabulary for Act I, scene ii and iii
6. To read Act I, scene ii and iii

Activity #1

Give students a few minutes to formulate answers for the study guide questions for Act I, scene i, and then discuss the answers to the questions in detail. Write the answers on the board or overhead transparency so students can have the correct answers for study purposes.

Note: It is a good practice in public speaking and leadership skills for individual students to take charge of leading the discussions of the study questions. Perhaps a different student could go to the front of the class and lead the discussion each day that the study questions are discussed during this unit. Of course, the teacher should guide the discussion when appropriate and be sure to fill in any gaps the students leave.

Activity #2

Distribute the non-fiction reading assignment sheet. Have students draw a slip from a hat/basket giving them the topic of their assignment.
Assignment Topics:
Shakespeare: The Early Years
Growing Up In Stratford-Upon-Avon
Shakespeare's Life In London
Elizabethan London
The Theatre: A Brief History
The Globe: The Workings Of The Stage
Elizabethan Audiences

Each student will complete a non-fiction reading assignment sheet based on his/her particular topic. In addition each student will write down at least FIVE interesting facts about their topic to share with the class. The class will be visiting the library/media center for the remainder of this lesson to work on the non-fiction assingment.

Activity #3

Tell students to preview the study questions, do the vocabulary worksheet, and read Act I, scene ii and iii prior to the next class meeting.

NONFICTION ASSIGNMENT SHEET

In addition to completing the nonfiction assignment sheet, on a separate sheet of paper, come up with at least FIVE interesting facts about your topic that you believe are important to share with the rest of the class.

(To be completed after reading the required nonfiction article)

Name _____ Date _____

Title of Nonfiction Read _____

Written By_____ Publication Date_____

I. Factual Summary: Write a short summary of the piece you read.

II. Vocabulary
    1. With which vocabulary words in the piece did you encounter some degree of difficulty?

    2. How did you resolve your lack of understanding with these words?

III. Interpretation: What was the main point the author wanted you to get from reading his work?

IV. Criticism
    1. With which points of the piece did you agree or find easy to accept? Why?

    2. With which points of the piece did you disagree or find difficult to believe? Why?

V. Personal Response: What do you think about this piece? OR How does this piece influence your ideas?

LESSON THREE

Objectives
1. To review the main events and ideas from Act I, scene ii and iii
2. To demonstrate reading comprehension by taking a quiz
3. To demonstrate knowledge of facts about Shakespeare's life and the Elizabethan theatre through sharing of facts gathered in library/media center
4. To improve oral reading skills through reading the play aloud
5. To improve dramatic/performance skills through performing the play
6. To practice note taking/critiquing skills while listening to others' presentations
7. To preview the study guide questions and vocabulary for Act II, scene i
8. To read Act II, scene i

Activity #1

Give students a few minutes to formulate answers for the study guide questions for Act I, scene ii and iii, and then discuss the answers to the questions in detail. Write the answers on the board or overhead transparency so students can have the correct answers for study purposes.

Activity #2

Quiz - Distribute quizzes for Act I and give students about 10 minutes to complete them.

Note: The quizzes may either be the short answer study guides or the multiple choice version. Have students exchange papers. Grade the quizzes as a class. Collect the papers for recording the grades. (If you used the multiple choice version as a quiz, take a few minutes to discuss the answers for the short answer version if your students are using the short answer version for their study guides.)

Activity #3

Have students who drew the same topic for the non-fiction assignment get together and share their findings (the five interesting facts about the topic that are worthy of sharing). Allow each group to present the facts they have gathered while all the rest of the students take notes. By the end of the sharing, all students will have information to help them better understand William Shakespeare's life and the Elizabethan theatre.

Activity #4

If possible move desks into a "U" shape (to allow for the illusion of a "thrust" stage). Students at their desks watch as Act I is acted out by the students selected in lesson 1. Each "audience member" is assigned a particular character to watch and critique. They are to make notes of performance skills and offer written feedback (three positive comments and two comments on how the performer could improve his/her performances in the future). Also, each student is to identify three specific traits that their assigned character seems to exhibit through his/her speeches.

Stop at the end of each scene to discuss the action and the events occurring. Selecting one character at a time, discuss the character traits identified by the "audience members." Be sure that each trait can be backed up with textual support.

Continue until the end of the act.

Assign parts for Act II to members of the audience, let them know they will be performing Act II in lesson 5. By the end of this unit, every student should have had the opportunity to perform at least once and to offer critiques to peers.

Note: Use the Evaluation Sheets and Critique Sheets from pages 72 and 73 in this LitPlan.

Activity #5
Tell students to preview the study questions, do the vocabulary worksheet, and read Act II, scene i prior to the next class meeting.

ORAL READING EVALUATION - *Much Ado About Nothing*

Name_____Class_____ Date _____

SKILL	EXCELLENT	GOOD	AVERAGE	FAIR	POOR
Fluency	5	4	3	2	1
Clarity	5	4	3	2	1
Audibility	5	4	3	2	1
Pronunciation	5	4	3	2	1
	5	4	3	2	1
	5	4	3	2	1

Total_____Grade_____

Comments:

PEER FEEDBACK - *Much Ado About Nothing*

Name of Critic: _____   Character: _____

Dear Fellow Thespian,

Thank you for your performance! I liked the way you:

1.

2.

3.

However, I would have liked to have seen the following included in your performance. Perhaps you could take these into consideration for future performances:

1.

2.

Based on what I heard from your character, I would say that he/she demonstrates the following traits (include textual reference):

1.

2.

3.

LESSON FOUR

Objectives
1. To review the main events and ideas from Act II, scene i
2. To understand the basic structure of a Shakespearean comedy
3. To give students the opportunity to practice creative writing by creating their own comedies
4. To work in cooperative groups to create their own comedies
5. To preview the study guide questions and vocabulary for Act II, scene ii and iii
6. To read Act II, scene ii and iii

Activity #1
Give students a few minutes to formulate answers for the study guide questions for Act II, scene i, and then discuss the answers to the questions in detail. Write the answers on the board or overhead transparency so students can have the correct answers for study purposes.

Activity #2
Break students into groups of six (or as close to six as possible). Distribute the Creative Writing Project sheets (see below) and discuss the directions in detail. They will be creating a three act play that follows the pattern of Shakespeare's comedies and contains the archetypal characters found in the Bard's plays.
Students are to begin brainstorming their projects and create an outline.

Basic Plot Line for a Shakespearean Comedy:
- Boy Meets Girl (and they immediately fall in love)
- Boy Loses Girl (either due to a misunderstanding or to a villain's machinations)
- Boy Gets Girl (a plan or a plot is concocted to get to the bottom of things and the two marry and live happily ever after)

This is usually done in five acts, but for our purposes, we will only do three.

Archetypal Characters:
- the girl (young, beautiful, usually easily manipulated as well as easily infatuated– most of the time, her father is involved in the plot)
- the boy (young, handsome, usually no parental units because he's on his own, also easily manipulated and easily infatuated)
- the villain (some jealous person who can't stand to see people happy together and decides to throw a monkey wrench into the deal)
- the "clown" (a person who provides comic relief whose purpose is to distract the audience from the sad state of affairs once things start to go wrong for the young couple. This heightens the sadness when the young couple is really on the rocks. Also, it is often the clown who, usually unwittingly, comes up with the solution to the problem.)

Songs
Shakespeare's comedies usually contain a variety of songs performed. These include:
- a prologue (usually a sonnet sung by a chorus. It gives the background information for the plot)
- a ditty (a short, witty song that is usually filled with sexual innuendoes)
- a lament (a sad song, usually over the death of a loved one)
- a love song (that's the obvious one; often in the form of a sonnet)

For your advanced students, you might challenge them to write in blank verse!

Activity #3
Tell students to preview the study questions, do the vocabulary worksheet, and read Act II, scene ii and iii prior to the next class meeting.

WRITING ASSIGNMENT #1 - *Much Ado About Nothing*
Creative - Writing a Shakespearean Comedy in Three Acts

PROMPT
Shakespeare's comedies usually follow this basic structure:
- Boy Meets Girl (and they immediately fall in love)
- Boy Loses Girl (either due to a misunderstanding or to a villain's machinations)
- Boy Gets Girl (a plan or a plot is concocted to get to the bottom of things and the two marry and live happily ever after)

This is usually done in five acts, but for our purposes, we will only do three.

The comedy also includes the following:
Archetypal Characters: the girl, the boy, the villain, the clown (among other characters)
Songs: a prologue, a ditty, a lament, a love song

Your group is to brainstorm a basic plot line that fits the Shakespearean pattern and:
- outline the chain of events (there will be three acts with two scenes per act)
- create characters (give character traits that will be consistent throughout the play; remember to create only as many characters as there are members of your group)
- design a setting
- create at least two songs to insert into the play

PREWRITING
Ideally, there are six people in a group. Each person is to choose which of the six scenes he/she would like to write. Since each scene must logically follow the preceding scene, it is imperative that students communicate. Also, it is important that specific character traits attributed during the brainstorming session are kept intact for each scene the character is in.

There will be a specific lesson for the songs, but each group is responsible for inserting at least two songs into its play. Students will collaborate on the creation of the songs.

DRAFTING
Considering the scope of your scene as well as the prior and following scenes, begin to write the stage directions and dialogue for the scene you are assigned. Remember to be true to your character's traits.

PROMPT
When you finish the rough draft of your section, ask another group member to read it. After reading your rough draft, he/she should tell you what he/she liked best about your work, which parts were difficult to understand, and ways in which your work could be improved. Be sure to look for logical progression for the whole play. Reread your paper considering your critic's comments, and make the corrections you think are necessary.

PROOFREADING
Do a final proofreading of your paper double-checking your grammar, spelling, organization, and the clarity of your ideas.

LESSON FIVE

Objectives
1. To review the main events and ideas from Act II, scene ii and iii
2. To demonstrate their understanding of Shakespeare's comedy through taking a quiz
3. To improve oral reading skills through reading the play aloud
4. To improve dramatic/performance skills through performing the play
5. To practice note taking/critiquing skills while listening to others' presentations
6. To preview the study guide questions and vocabulary for Act III, scene i and ii
7. To read Act III, scene i and ii

Activity #1

Give students a few minutes to formulate answers for the study guide questions for Act II, scenes ii and iii, and then discuss the answers to the questions in detail. Write the answers on the board or overhead transparency so students can have the correct answers for study purposes.

Activity #2

Quiz - Distribute quizzes for Act II and give students about 10 minutes to complete them.

Note: The quizzes may either be the short answer study guides or the multiple choice version. Have students exchange papers. Grade the quizzes as a class. Collect the papers for recording the grades. (If you used the multiple choice version as a quiz, take a few minutes to discuss the answers for the short answer version if your students are using the short answer version for their study guides.)

Activity #3

The desks should already be set into a "U" shape (to allow for the illusion of a "thrust" stage). Students at their desks watch as Act II is acted out by the students selected the day before. Each "audience member" is assigned a particular character to watch and critique. They are to make notes of performance skills and offer written feedback (three positive comments and two comments on how the performer could improve his/her performances in the future). Also, each student is to identify three specific traits that their assigned character seems to exhibit through his/her speeches.

Stop at the end of each scene to discuss the action and the events occurring. Selecting one character at a time, discuss the character traits identified by the "audience members." Be sure that each trait can be backed up with textual support.

Continue until the end of the act.

Assign parts for Act III to members of the audience, let them know they will be performing Act II in lesson 7 . By then end of this unit, every student should have had the opportunity to perform at least once and to offer critiques to peers.

Note: Use the Evaluation Sheets and Critique Sheets from pages 72 and 73 in this LitPlan.

Activity #4

Tell students to preview the study questions, do the vocabulary worksheet, and read Act III, scene i and ii prior to the next class meeting.

LESSON SIX

<u>Objectives</u>
1. To review the main events and ideas from Act III, scene i and ii
2. To improve social/cooperative skills through working in creative writing groups
3. To preview the study guide questions and vocabulary for Act III, scene ii through v
4. To read Act III, scene ii through v

<u>Activity #1</u>
Give students a few minutes to formulate answers for the study guide questions for Act III, scenes i and ii, and then discuss the answers to the questions in detail. Write the answers on the board or overhead transparency so students can have the correct answers for study purposes.

<u>Activity #2</u>
Allow students to continue with their group creative writing projects. Go around and listen to their ideas, offering suggestions/feedback as necessary.

<u>Activity #3</u>
Tell students to preview the study questions, do the vocabulary worksheet, and read Act III, scene ii through v prior to the next class meeting.

LESSON SEVEN

Objectives
1. To review the main events and ideas from Act III, scene iii through v
2. To demonstrate their understanding of Shakespeare's comedy through taking a quiz
3. To improve oral reading skills through reading the play aloud
4. To improve dramatic/performance skills through performing the play
5. To practice note taking/critiquing skills while listening to others' presentations
6. To preview the study guide questions and vocabulary for Act IV, scene i
7. To read Act IV, scene i

Activity #1

Give students a few minutes to formulate answers for the study guide questions for Act III, scenes iii and v, and then discuss the answers to the questions in detail. Write the answers on the board or overhead transparency so students can have the correct answers for study purposes.

Activity #2

Quiz - Distribute quizzes for Act III and give students about 10 minutes to complete them.

Note: The quizzes may either be the short answer study guides or the multiple choice version. Have students exchange papers. Grade the quizzes as a class. Collect the papers for recording the grades. (If you used the multiple choice version as a quiz, take a few minutes to discuss the answers for the short answer version if your students are using the short answer version for their study guides.)

Activity #3

The desks should already be set into a "U" shape (to allow for the illusion of a "thrust" stage). Students at their desks watch as Act III is acted out by the students selected the day before. Each "audience member" is assigned a particular character to watch and critique. They are to make notes of performance skills and offer written feedback (three positive comments and two comments on how the performer could improve his/her performances in the future). Also, each student is to identify three specific traits that their assigned character seems to exhibit through his/her speeches.
Stop at the end of each scene to discuss the action and the events occurring. Selecting one character at a time, discuss the character traits identified by the "audience members." Be sure that each trait can be backed up with textual support.
Continue until the end of the act.
Assign parts for IV to members of the audience. By the end of this unit, every student should have had the opportunity to perform at least once and to offer critiques to peers.

Note: Use the Evaluation Sheets and Critique Sheets from pages 72 and 73 in this LitPlan.

Activity #4

Tell students to preview the study questions, do the vocabulary worksheet, and read Act IV, scene i prior to the next class meeting.

LESSON EIGHT

Objectives
1. To review the main events and ideas from Act IV, scene i
2. To practice writing to inform
3. To preview the study guide questions and vocabulary for Act IV, scene ii
4. To read Act IV, scene ii

Activity #1
  Give students a few minutes to formulate answers for the study guide questions for Act IV, scene i, and then discuss the answers to the questions in detail. Write the answers on the board or overhead transparency so students can have the correct answers for study purposes.

Activity #2
  Distribute Writing Assignment #2 (a research assignment) and discuss the directions in detail. Then take students to the library/media center for research work.

Activity #3
  Tell students to preview the study questions, do the vocabulary worksheet, and read Act IV, scene ii prior to the next class meeting.

WRITING ASSIGNMENT #2 - *Much Ado About Nothing*
Informational: Changes to the Theatre brought about by Charles II

PROMPT
You are reading Shakespeare's comedy *Much Ado About Nothing*, and the class has been exploring elements of Shakespeare's theatre as you read/perform. After the return of King Charles II from his long exile in France, this enthusiastic theatre-lover brought ideas from the theatres of France and implemented changes in the theatre of England. Research Charles II and his innovative ideas that he brought to the English stage.

After researching the required information at the library/media center, use your findings to write a report on three specific ideas that Charles II brought with him from France that changed the English theatre forever. You must support your ideas with quotations from your sources and cite them correctly.

PREWRITING
Use any resources available in the library/media center to find out what ideas Charles II brought to the English stage. Take notes of important facts as you read. Be sure to note the sources of your facts so they can be acknowledged appropriately in your essay.

DRAFTING
Introduce your topic in the first paragraph, being sure to end with a thesis statement. Then write several body paragraphs, each describing a different idea that Charles II brought to the English stage. Be sure to include embedded quotations from your research as support for your thesis. Also, incorporate at least four vocabulary words from the unit into your essay. Finally, conclude by making modern connections to those involved in the entertainment industry who have made significant contributions to positive changes in the entertainment business (theatre/films/television). End the conclusion by challenging your reader in some way.

PEER CONFERENCE/REVISING
When you finish the draft, ask another student to look at it. You may want to give the student your worksheets and articles so he/she can double check to see you have included all the information you intended to include. After reading, he/she should tell you what is best about your essay, which parts were difficult to understand or follow, and ways in which your essay could be improved. Reread your essay considering your critic's comments and make the corrections you think are necessary.

PROOFREADING/EDITING
Do a final proofreading of your essay, double-checking your grammar, spelling, organization, and the clarity of your ideas.

WRITING EVALUATION FORM - Much Ado About Nothing

Name_____ Date _____

Grade _____

Circle One For Each Item:

Grammar:	correct		errors noted on paper	
Spelling:	correct		errors noted on paper	
Punctuation:	correct		errors noted on paper	
Legibility:	excellent	good	fair	poor
	excellent	good	fair	poor
	excellent	good	fair	poor

Strengths:

Weaknesses:

Comments/Suggestions:

LESSON NINE

Objectives
1. To review the main events and ideas from Act IV, scene ii
2. To demonstrate their understanding of Shakespeare's comedy through taking a quiz
3. To improve oral reading skills through reading the play aloud
4. To improve dramatic/performance skills through performing the play
5. To practice note taking/critiquing skills while listening to others' presentations
6. To preview the study guide questions and vocabulary for Act V, scene i
7. To read Act V, scene i

Activity #1
  Give students a few minutes to formulate answers for the study guide questions for Act IV, scene ii, and then discuss the answers to the questions in detail. Write the answers on the board or overhead transparency so students can have the correct answers for study purposes.

Activity #2
  Quiz - Distribute quizzes for Act IV and give students about 10 minutes to complete them.

Note: The quizzes may either be the short answer study guides or the multiple choice version. Have students exchange papers. Grade the quizzes as a class. Collect the papers for recording the grades. (If you used the multiple choice version as a quiz, take a few minutes to discuss the answers for the short answer version if your students are using the short answer version for their study guides.)

Activity #3
  The desks should already be set into a "U" shape (to allow for the illusion of a "thrust" stage). Students at their desks watch as Act IV is acted out by the students selected the day before. Each "audience member" is assigned a particular character to watch and critique. They are to make notes of performance skills and offer written feedback (three positive comments and two comments on how the performer could improve his/her performances in the future). Also, each student is to identify three specific traits that their assigned character seems to exhibit through his/her speeches.
  Stop at the end of each scene to discuss the action and the events occurring. Selecting one character at a time, discuss the character traits identified by the "audience members." Be sure that each trait can be backed up with textual support.
  Continue until the end of the act. Assign parts for Act V to members of the audience, be sure to tell them they will be performing Act V in lesson 11. By the end of this unit, every student should have had the opportunity to perform at least once and to offer critiques to peers.

Note: Use the Evaluation Sheets and Critique Sheets from pages 72 and 73 in this LitPlan

Activity #4
  Tell students to preview the study questions, do the vocabulary worksheet, and read Act V, scene i prior to the next class meeting.

LESSON TEN

Objectives
1. To review the main events and ideas from Act V, scene i
2. To become familiar with the structure of a Shakespearean sonnet
3. To become familiar with other types of songs that Shakespeare used in his comedies and demonstrate the ability to insert them into their own comedies
4. To preview the study guide questions and vocabulary for Act V, scene ii through iv
5. To read Act V, scene ii through iv

Activity #1
   Give students a few minutes to formulate answers for the study guide questions for Act V, scene i, and then discuss the answers to the questions in detail. Write the answers on the board or overhead transparency so students can have the correct answers for study purposes.

Activity #2
   Distribute copies of Shakespeare's prologue from *Romeo and Juliet* (see below). As was done with the blank verse on Day 1, students will break the sonnet into its appropriate lines by recognizing the use of iambic pentameter; however, they have the additional clue that there is a particular rhyme scheme to help them. Allow students to break the sonnet into lines and then try to identify the pattern of rhyme on their own.
   After they have completed the activity, be sure to point out the specific rhyme scheme of a Shakespearean sonnet (a,b,a,b,c,d,c,d,e,f,e,f,g,g) and that each line is written in iambic pentameter.
   Also, ask the students what the function of the prologue seems to be for the play *Romeo and Juliet.* (It sets the scene, gives background information about the plot, foreshadows the events that are about to occur on the stage)

Activity #3
   Shakespeare also wrote ditties (witty songs that often, but not always, contained sexual innuendoes: playful), laments (songs of woe from the loss of a loved one), and love songs. Examine the three songs from Shakespeare's *Much Ado About Nothing* (see worksheets below) and determine how each fits into its particular category. Discuss the poetic devices or uses of rhetorical language Shakespeare used in each to create its intended effect.

Activity #4
   Have students get into their creative writing groups and they must decide which two of the four types of songs will be included in their own productions. They must collaborate on the creation of the two songs (since there are six students to a group, it might be a good idea to have three work on each of the two songs).

Activity #5
   Tell students to preview the study questions, do the vocabulary worksheet, and read Act V, scene ii through iv prior to the next class meeting.

Shakespeare's Prologue from *Romeo and Juliet*

Break the prose lines below into their poetic form. Remember that each line is written in iambic pentameter, so do not be afraid to bang the beat out on your desks while you break this into its proper lines. Once you have finished, examine the lines and see if there is any pattern of rhyme that can be identified.

Two households, both alike in dignity, in fair Verona, where we lay our scene, from ancient grudge break to new mutiny, where civil blood makes civil hands unclean. From forth the fatal loins of these two foes a pair of star-cross'd lovers take their life; whose misadventur'd piteous overthrows doth with their death bury their parents' strife. The fearful passage of their death-mark'd love, and the continuance of their parents' rage, which, but their children's end, nought could remove, is now the two hours' traffic of our stage; the which if you with patient ears attend, what here shall miss, our toil shall strive to mend.

Proper line format:

What do you notice (if anything) about any particular rhyming patterns?

ANSWER KEY Shakespeare's Prologue from *Romeo and Juliet* (in its sonnet format)

Two households, both alike in dignity,
In fair Verona, where we lay our scene,
From ancient grudge break to new mutiny,
Where civil blood makes civil hands unclean.
From forth the fatal loins of these two foes
A pair of star-cross'd lovers take their life;
Whose misadventur'd piteous overthrows
Doth with their death bury their parents' strife.
The fearful passage of their death-mark'd love,
And the continuance of their parents' rage,
Which, but their children's end, nought could remove,
Is now the two hours' traffic of our stage;
The which if you with patient ears attend,
What here shall miss, our toil shall strive to mend.

Songs from *Much Ado About Nothing*

Act II, scene iii:

Balthasar:

> Sigh no more, ladies, sigh no more,
> Men were deceivers ever,
> One foot in sea and one on shore,
> To one thing constant never:
> Then sigh not so, but let them go,
> And be you blithe and bonny,
> Converting all your sounds of woe
> Into Hey nonny, nonny.
> Sing no more ditties, sing no moe,
> Of dumps so dull and heavy;
> The fraud of men was ever so,
> Since summer first was leafy:
> Then sigh not so, & c.

What type of song is this? _____

What makes you think so? _____

What is this song about? _____

How does this song fit into the plot of *Much Ado About Nothing*?

_____

_____

What poetic/rhetorical devices can you find in this song that help create the specific nature of the song?

_____

_____

_____

Songs from *Much Ado About Nothing* page 2

Act V, scene 3:

Balthasar:

> Pardon, goddess of the night,
> Those that slew thy virgin knight;
> For the which, with songs of woe,
> Round about her tomb they go.
> Midnight, assist our moan;
> Help us to sigh and groan,
> Heavily, heavily:
> Graves, yawn and yield your dead,
> Till death be uttered,
> Heavily, heavily.

What type of song is this? _____

What makes you think so? _____

What is this song about? _____

How does this song fit into the plot of *Much Ado About Nothing*?

_____

_____

What poetic/rhetorical devices can you find in this song that help create the specific nature of the song?

_____

_____

Songs from *Much Ado About Nothing* page 3

Act V, scene ii:

Benedick:

    The gods of love that sits about
            and know me, and know me,
                    how sorrowful I do serve,
    grant my request that at the least,
            she show me, she show me,
                    some pity when I deserve;
    that every brawl may turn to bliss,
            to joy with all that joyful is.
                    Do this my dear and bind me
    forever and ever your own;
            And as you here do find me
                    so let your love be shown,
    for till I hear this unity
            I languish in extremity.

    As yet I have a soul to save
            uprightly, uprightly;
                    though troubled with despair,
    I cannot find to set my mind
            so lightly, so lightly,
                    as die before you be there.
    But since I must needs you provoke,
            come slake the thirst, stand by the stroke,
    that when my heart is fainted
            the sorrowful signs may tell
    you might have been acquainted
            with one that loved you well.
    None have I told the jeopardy
            that none but you can remedy...

    With courtesy now so bend, so bow,
            to speed me, to speed me,
                    an answereth my desire;
    as I will be if ever I see
            you need, you need me,
                    as ready when you require.
    Unworthy though to come so nigh
            that passing show that feeds mine eye,
    yet shall I die without it
            if pity be not in you.
                    But sure I can not doubt it
    nor anything you can do–
    to whom I do commit, and shall,
            my self to work your will with all.

Songs from *Much Ado About Nothing* page 4

What type of song is this? _____

What makes you think so? _____

What is this song about? _____

How does this song fit into the plot of *Much Ado About Nothing*?

_____

_____

What poetic/rhetorical devices can you find in this song that help create the specific nature of the song?

_____

_____

LESSON ELEVEN

Objectives
1. To review the main events and ideas from Act V, scene ii through iv
2. To demonstrate their understanding of Shakespeare's comedy through taking a quiz
3. To improve oral reading skills through reading the play aloud
4. To improve dramatic/performance skills through performing the play
5. To practice note taking/critiquing skills while listening to others' presentations

Activity #1
Give students a few minutes to formulate answers for the study guide questions for Act V, scene ii through iv, and then discuss the answers to the questions in detail. Write the answers on the board or overhead transparency so students can have the correct answers for study purposes.

Activity #2
Quiz - Distribute quizzes for Act V and give students about 10 minutes to complete them.

Note: The quizzes may either be the short answer study guides or the multiple choice version. Have students exchange papers. Grade the quizzes as a class. Collect the papers for recording the grades. (If you used the multiple choice version as a quiz, take a few minutes to discuss the answers for the short answer version if your students are using the short answer version for their study guides.)

Activity #3
The desks should already be set into a "U" shape (to allow for the illusion of a "thrust" stage). Students at their desks watch as Act V is acted out by the students selected the day before. Each "audience member" is assigned a particular character to watch and critique. They are to make notes of performance skills and offer written feedback (three positive comments and two comments on how the performer could improve his/her performances in the future). Also, each student is to identify three specific traits that their assigned character seems to exhibit through his/her speeches.

Stop at the end of each scene to discuss the action and the events occurring. Selecting one character at a time, discuss the character traits identified by the "audience members." Be sure that each trait can be backed up with textual support.

Continue until the end of the act. This will complete the oral reading of *Much Ado About Nothing*.

Note: Use the Evaluation Sheets and Critique Sheets from pages 72 and 73 in this LitPlan

LESSON TWELVE

Objectives
1. To introduce the role of the clown or comic relief
2. To work in collaborative groups, to work on their creative project

Activity #1

Ask students to brainstorm ideas about clowns and write responses on the board. (Probably, the circus clown will be the one that will pop up most quickly into the students' minds). Other ideas might include: rodeo clowns, mimes, comedians in television and movies (Robin Williams, Will Farrell, Jim Carey, Jerry Seinfeld, etc.)

Put students into their creative writing groups, and ask them to discuss what they think the role/purpose of a clown is (in general). Tell them to go beyond the obvious: to make people laugh. After a few minutes, share responses. If the following are not included in student responses, lead them to "discover" the following:

* clowns point out human weaknesses that we all face; they help people not to take themselves so seriously (ex. Seinfeld was touted as a show about "nothing", yet Jerry, George, Elaine and Kramer exhibited the "quirky" side of human nature that exists in all of us).
* clowns comment on social/political issues and make people think ABOUT those issues (satirists, *South Park*, *The Simpsons*)
* clowns temporarily relieve the tension of perilous events in order to give the audience a "rest" from the tension (rodeo and circus clowns): comic relief
* clowns are sometimes a voice of reason in a tragedy; he makes the tragic character seem all the more tragic (King Lear's Fool)

Ask students to discuss Dogberry's role in *Much Ado About Nothing*. Why do they think this character is included in the plot? What function does he serve?

For their comedies, students must include a "clown" character that will fill one of the above functions.

Activity #2

Students will continue working on their comedies, being sure that at least one of their characters function as the role of "comic relief" or a "clown."

LESSON THIRTEEN

<u>Objective</u>
    To review all of the vocabulary work done in this unit

<u>Activity</u>
    Choose one (or more) of the vocabulary review activities listed below and spend your class period as directed in the activity. Some of the materials for these review activities are l located in the Vocabulary Resource Materials section in this LitPlan.

VOCABULARY REVIEW ACTIVITIES

1. Divide your class into two teams and have an old-fashioned spelling or definition bee.

2. Give each of your students (or students in groups of two, three or four) a *Much Ado About Nothing* Vocabulary Word Search Puzzle. The person (group) to find all of the vocabulary words in the puzzle first wins.

3. Give students a *Much Ado About Nothing* Vocabulary Word Search Puzzle without the word list. The person or group to find the most vocabulary words in the puzzle wins.

4. Use a *Much Ado About Nothing* Vocabulary Crossword Puzzle. Put the puzzle onto a transparency on the overhead projector (so everyone can see it), and do the puzzle together as a class.

5. Give students a *Much Ado About Nothing* Vocabulary Matching Worksheet to do.

6. Divide your class into two teams. Use *Much Ado About Nothing* vocabulary words with their letters jumbled as a word list. Student 1 from Team A faces off against Student 1 from Team B. You write the first jumbled word on the board. The first student (1A or 1B) to unscramble the word wins the chance for his/her team to score points. If 1A wins the jumble, go to student 2A and give him/her a definition. He/she must give you the correct spelling of the vocabulary word which fits that definition. If he/she does, Team A scores a point, and you give student 3A a definition for which you expect a correctly spelled matching vocabulary word. Continue giving Team A definitions until some team member makes an incorrect response. An incorrect response sends the game back to the jumbled-word face off, this time with students 2A and 2B. Instead of repeating giving definitions to the first few students of each team, continue with the student after the one who gave the last incorrect response on the team. For example, if Team B wins the jumbled-word face-off, and student 5B gave the last incorrect answer for Team B, you would start this round of definition questions with student 6B, and so on. The team with the most points wins!

7. Play "I Have... Who Has?" This requires advance preparation, but the students really seem to enjoy it. Using your entire vocabulary list from *Much Ado About Nothing*, create a set of cards where the definition for the first word is written on the first card, but the word that goes WITH the definition is written on the second card. On the BACK of the second card, write the definition for the second word, and on the third card, write the second word... continue until you come to the end of the list. Write the final word on the back of the first card that has definition #1. (The whole set will create an entire loop of vocabulary words). Shuffle the cards and distribute among the students, keeping one for yourself. Have students put the cards on their desks with the word facing UP. You then say, "Who has..." and read the definition on the back of the card. Whichever student who has the card with the correct vocabulary word that matches the definition calls out, "I have..." and reads the word. He/She then flips that card over and says, "Who has..." and reads the definition. The game continues until the loop returns with the card in the teacher's hand matches the last definition read. You can use a stop watch and get various classes try to beat the best times.

8. Have students write a story in which they correctly use as many vocabulary words as possible. Have students read their compositions orally! Post the most original compositions on your bulletin board!

LESSON FOURTEEN

Objective
    To discuss the play on a deeper level

Activity
    Choose the questions from the Extra Discussion Questions/Writing Assignments which seem most appropriate for your students. A class discussion of these questions is most effective if students have been given the opportunity to formulate answers to the questions prior to the discussion. To this end, you may either have all the students formulate answers to all the questions, divide your class into groups and assign one or more questions to each group, or you could assign one question to each student in your class. The option you choose will make a difference in the amount of class time needed for this activity. The class discussion of these questions is scheduled for Lesson Fifteen.

    NOTE: The use of graphic organizers may be helpful to students in preparing their answers. Encourage them to use any diagrams or graphics that they feel are necessary.

EXTRA WRITING ASSIGNMENTS/DISCUSSION QUESTIONS -
Much Ado About Nothing

Interpretation
1. Attribute two negative and two positive character traits for each of the following:
   a. Beatrice
   b. Benedick
   c. Claudio
   d. Hero
   e. Don Pedro
   f. Leonato

   Be sure to support each trait with specific evidence from the text.
2. What has brought about Benedick's change of attitude toward marriage as evidenced by his final words to Don Pedro?
3. Examine Dogberry's confusion of words throughout his scenes. What words does he really intend to use, but doesn't?
4. What are the main conflicts in the play? Are they all resolved by the end of the play?
5. Where is the high point (cliamx) of the play?
6. What is the setting, and how does it add to the play?

Critical
1. Examine the relationship between Don Pedro and Don John. To what might you be able to contribute the animosity between them?
2. When Beatrice claims that she "knows [Benedick] of old," what does this suggest about the animosity between them?
3. Does Claudio really love Hero? Give textual evidence to support your answer.
4. Do Beatrice and Benedick really love one anther? Support your answer with evidence from the text.
5. Note that Claudio is not filled with remorse at the news that Hero has died. He only feels regret once Borachio confesses to the plot. Even then, Claudio claims that his only sin was in mistaking Margaret for Hero. What does this show about Claudio's character?
6. Note the fact that when Don John tells Claudio that Don Pedro is attempting to woo Hero for himself, Claudio instantly berates Hero in his speeches by saying that "beauty is a witch." Moments later, Don Pedro breaks the news to Claudio that Hero has been won for him, and once again, his attitude toward Hero immediately changes to happiness. What do these instances demonstrate about Claudio's character?
7. When Hero is denounced by Claudio in the church, Leonato immediately believes Claudio's accusations and wishes that his daughter was dead. What does this say about his character? What seems to be his biggest concern surrounding the scandal?
8. In Act II, scene i, lines 16-17, Leonato proclaims, "By my troth, niece, thou wilt never get a husband if thou be so shrewd of thy tongue". What is he saying about the roles of women in a relationship? Whose attitude is it that women should not be "so shrewd (clever) of... tongue"? Do these men seem to be threatened by strong women? Explain.
9. Examine the irony of the fact that marital advice/machinations are concocted by men who have taken a vow to never marry.

Critical/Personal Response
1. When Claudio was attacking Hero in the church, why do you suppose Beatrice didn't speak up to defend her? Beatrice claims that she and Hero have been sharing a bed for over a year. Wouldn't she have noticed if Hero had taken a lover?
2. Why do you suppose Beatrice and Benedick were so easily taken in by the plot to bring them together? What does this suggest about the "merry war" between them?
3. Many women in today's society are abused by their significant others. Why do you suppose Hero still wants to marry Claudio even after he treated he so badly at the

church? What could her decision to continue to stay with him say about women in general?
4. Hero is a most obedient daughter who does whatever her father tells her to. What does this say about the role between fathers and daughters in Elizabethan times? How have the relationships between fathers and daughters changed in the time since?
5. Examine the relationship between men and women in *Much Ado About Nothing*. What does each relationship (Hero/Claudio, Beatrice/Benedick, and Margaret/Borachio) demonstrate about gender roles in Elizabethan society? Have these gender roles changed in the time since? Give reasons to support your answer.
6. In *Romeo and Juliet*, it is Friar Lawrence who comes up with the plan to keep the two lovers together. Friar Francis plays a similar role in *Much Ado About Nothing*. Consider what Shakespeare's attitudes might be about the role of the clergy in Elizabethan times.
7. Suppose Claudio had not been remorseful after hearing Borachio's confession. What would have become of Hero? How might she feel about the situation?
8. Why do you suppose Hero faints at Claudio's accusation instead of getting angry and stalking out of the church? Would the situation have been different if it had been Benedick who accused Beatrice? Explain.
9. Suppose that Hero pretended to go along with the Friar's plot and then, when all was to "be set right" between Hero and Claudio at the church, she denounced him for the idiot he is, slapped him in the face and left him at the altar with his mouth hanging open. How might the other characters react? Who might be on Hero's side? Who would take Claudio's side? Explain.
10. Much of the action of *Much Ado About Nothing* is propelled by the fact that certain characters "happen" to overhear what others are saying. Benedick eavesdrops on a conversation between Don Pedro and Claudio. Beatrice "accidentally" overhears what Hero and Margaret say about Benedick's feelings for her. Don John "hears" from an outside "source" that Don Pedro is wooing Hero for himself and share this "truth" with Claudio. What social comments might Shakespeare be making about eavesdropping and rumors? It has been suggested by critics that the play was originally titled *Much Ado About Noting* (as in "noting" what one hears from others).. Would this have been a more appropriate title? Explain why or why not.

Personal Response
1. In Act II, scene iii, Benedick makes a list of all the qualities that he is looking for in a woman. What qualities do you look for in a boyfriend/girlfriend?
2. Which character would you most like to play if you were cast in *Much Ado About Nothing*? Why?
3. Which character would you be the most unhappy about being cast as by a director? Why?
4. How do you react when you have been accused of something you didn't do?
5. Suppose you happened to hear that someone you have consistently shown a dislike for was really in love with you. How would you react to the news?
6. Don Pedro concocts a plot to bring Beatrice and Benedick together. Have you ever tried to "fix up" any of your friends with potential boyfriends/girlfriends? How did it turn out? Think of two people you know who don't really know (or even like) each other. How might you go about bringing them together? What do you think the result might be?
7. Have you or anyone you know ever been the target of being "hooked up" with someone unwittingly? How did you/he/she feel once the truth about being pushed together come to light? If you haven't experienced this, imagine what you might feel like if some of your friends did it to you.

LESSON FIFTEEN

<u>Objectives</u>
      1. To work in collaborative groups as they prepare for their performances
      2. To select appropriate costumes and props for their upcoming performances

<u>Activity</u>
    Students will break into their groups for last minute polishing and preparation. They must decide on costumes for characters as well as generate a prop list. They should also decide what scenery (desks, chairs, etc) will be needed for their performances.

    After they finish the last minute planning, the rest of the time should be spent in rehearsal. It is expected that the students memorize their lines.

LESSON SIXTEEN

<u>Objectives</u>
    To practice writing to persuade
    To further analyze the main characters in the play

<u>Activity #1</u>
    Distribute Writing Assignment #3 to each student and discuss the directions in detail. Give students the remaining time to write the essay in class.

<u>Activity #2</u>
    In the event students finish early, they may work on more of the Extra Discussion Questions or work independently editing their portion of the tragedy written in groups.

WRITING ASSIGNMENT #3 - *Much Ado About Nothing*
Persuasive: Happily Ever After?

PROMPT
You have finished reading the Shakespearean comedy *Much Ado About Nothing*, and the class has been observing the interactions between the couples in the play. Which couple's relationship will stand the test of time: Hero and Claudio or Beatrice and Benedick? Your assignment is to write a persuasive essay convincing me which couple's relationship will last.

PREWRITING
You must describe the relationships of BOTH couples before deciding which of the two has the best chance of survival in married life. Make a chart of pros and cons for each relationship before making your final choice. Each pro and con must be evidence from the text as support for your argument.

DRAFTING
Introduce your topic in the first paragraph, being sure to end with a thesis statement. The introduction should introduce both couples and your thesis should mention which you believe has the longest staying power. In your body paragraphs, you must give two specific reasons why your chosen couple WILL survive the test of time. These will be your first two body paragraphs (one paragraph for each). Don't forget to embed quotations from the play as evidence for your argument. Your next two body paragraphs will explain why the other couple will NOT survive. Again, you must present textual evidence for support. Be sure to incorporate at least four vocabulary words from the unit into your essay. End the conclusion by challenging your reader in some way.

PEER CONFERENCE/REVISING
When you finish the draft, ask another student to look at it. You may want to give the student your pre-writing notes and scenario so he/she can double check to see you have included all the information you intended to include. After reading, he/she should tell you what is best about your essay, which parts were difficult to understand or follow, and ways in which your essay could be improved. Reread your essay considering your critic's comments and make the corrections you think are necessary. You will be completing a peer editing form the next class.

PROOFREADING/EDITING
Do a final proofreading of your essay, double-checking your grammar, spelling, organization, and the clarity of your ideas.

SEVENTEEN

<u>Objectives</u>
1. To demonstrate the ability to assess another's writing thorough a peer editing exercise
2. To demonstrate the ability to accept constructive criticism and make changes in their writing when necessary

<u>Activity #1</u>
Put students in pairs for peer editing and give each student a peer evaluation form. Students will exchange their persuasive essays written in class the day before and make comments regarding content, language use, and conventions (under "Editor"). Students will return the essays to the writer and then they respond to their peer's comments about their own writing on the editing sheet (under "Writer"). After thanking his/her peer for their comments, the writer will revise and rewrite the essay to turn in for a grade.

<u>Activity #2</u>
Once students have edited and revised their writing and turned the essays in to be graded, they may work on finishing their projects for the upcoming presentations.

Editor's Name _____ Date _____

Writer's Name _____ Assignment _____

Peer Editing for Writing Assignments

A. Was the writer's position clearly stated?

If your answer is "yes," be sure to tell the writer what he/she did that you especially liked. If your answer is "no," tell the writer what he/she could have included in order to write a better essay.

Editor: _____

_____

_____

Writer: _____

_____

_____

B. Did he/she provide enough details to support his/her position?

If your answer is "yes," be sure to tell the writer what you especially liked about his/her response. If your answer is "no," you must tell the writer how he/she could improve his/her response (adding specific details that were missed, connecting to position better, or adding embedded quotations).

Editor: _____

_____

_____

Writer: _____

_____

_____

C. Identify sentence type

Be sure to know the difference between simple, simple with compound subject, simple with compound predicate, compound, complex, and compound-complex. Using the first body paragraph, correctly identify each sentence type. If there is sufficient sentence structure variety, tell the writer what he/she did well. If not, explain what he/she could have done differently.

Sentence 1: _____   Sentence 5: _____

Sentence 2: _____   Sentence 6: _____

Sentence 3: _____   Sentence 7: _____

Sentence 4: _____   Sentence 8: _____

Editor: _____

_____

Writer: _____

_____

D. Address the Focus Correction Areas

Did the writer follow the specifics of the essay such as (address each individually):

Organization:
Editor:
_____

Writer:
_____

Use of vocabulary words as directed:
Editor:
_____

Writer:
_____

Cite play when referring to characters in Much Ado About Nothing:
Editor:
_____

Writer:
_____

E. Check for errors in grammar, spelling, punctuation, etc.

Editor:
_____

Writer:
_____

LESSONS EIGHTEEN AND NINETEEN

<u>Objectives</u>
    1. To practice public speaking skills through the presentations of their group tragedies
    2. To demonstrate the structure of a Greek tragedy through their presentations

<u>Activity #1</u>
    There will probably be time for two or three of the groups to present each day. Distribute enough copies for each student to evaluate the plays that they will be watching being performed. Each student will evaluate the group's presentation and provide feedback for their peers. The teacher, of course, will be evaluating as well. A group presentation evaluation sheet has been provided for your convenience.

<u>Activity #2</u>
    If there is any remaining time, the teacher can provide further vocabulary review materials or any of the other review materials in preparation for the unit test.

Group Presentation Evaluation Sheet

Each of the following will be graded on a scale of 1-5, with 1 being the lowest; each is worth 20% of the overall grade.

Part I: Individual contribution during the preparation time in class (This has been monitored during media center visit and in-class group work)

Part II: Individual contribution to the group project/performance (how well he/she has memorized or is at least prepared to read from a script his/her part)

Part III: Individual contributed correct format to the class based on the structure of a Shakespearean Comedy

Part IV: Individual portion of the play remains consistent with rest of play

Part V: Individual has provided all of his/her necessary portion of the group project (this includes the song)

Title: _____

Student Name	Part I	Part II	Part III	Part IV	Part V	Total Score

Write all comments on the back of this sheet.

LESSON TWENTY

Objective
 To review the main ideas and events in *Much Ado About Nothing*

Activity #1
 Choose one of the following review games/activities and spend your class time as directed there.

1. Ask the class to make up a unit test for *Much Ado About Nothing*. The test should have 4 sections: matching, true/false, short answer, and essay. Students may use 1/2 period to make the test and then swap papers and use the other 1/2 class period to take a test a classmate has devised. (open book) You may want to use the unit test included in this packet or take questions from the students' unit tests to formulate your own test.

2. Take 1/2 period for students to make up true and false questions (including the answers). Collect the papers and divide the class into two teams. Draw a big tic-tac-toe board on the chalk board. Make one team X and one team O. Ask questions to each side, giving each student one turn. If the question is answered correctly, that students' team's letter (X or O) is placed in the box. If the answer is incorrect, no letter is placed in the box. The object is to get three in a row like tic-tac-toe. You may want to keep track of the number of games won for each team.

3. Take 1/2 period for students to make up questions (true/false and short answer). Collect the questions. Divide the class into two teams. You'll alternate asking questions to individual members of teams A & B (like in a spelling bee). The question keeps going from A to B until it is correctly answered, then a new question is asked. A correct answer does not allow the team to get another question. Correct answers are +2 points; incorrect answers are -1 point.

4. Have students pair up and quiz each other from their study guides and class notes.

5. Give students a *Much Ado About Nothing* crossword puzzle to complete.

6. Divide your class into two teams. Use *Much Ado About Nothing* crossword words with their letters jumbled as a word list. Student 1 from Team A faces off against Student 1 from Team B. You write the first jumbled word on the board. The first student (1A or 1B) to unscramble the word wins the chance for his/her team to score points. If 1A wins the jumble, go to student 2A and give him/her a clue. He/she must give you the correct word which matches that clue. If he/she does, Team A scores a point, and you give student 3A a clue for which you expect another correct response. Continue giving Team A clues until some team member makes an incorrect response. An incorrect response sends the game back to the jumbled-word face off, this time with students 2A and 2B. Instead of repeating giving clues to the first few students of each team, continue with the student after the one who gave the last incorrect response on the team. For example, if Team B wins the jumbled-word face-off, and student 5B gave the last incorrect answer for Team B, you would start this round of clue questions with student 6B, and so on. The team with the most points wins!

Review Games Page 2

8. Play *What's My Line?*. This is similar to the old television show. Students assume the roles of different characters from the epic. One student gives clues to the class, or to a panel of contestants. The contestants try to guess the identity of the guest. Students may enjoy assisting you in creating rules and procedures for the game.

9. Play *Jeopardy*. Divide the class into two groups. Assign each group a category or book from the epic and have them devise answers for that category. Play the game according to the television show procedures.

10. Play Drawing in the Details. This is similar to Pictionary. Divide students into teams. A student from one team draws a scene from the epic. (You may want to specify the Book or section.) Drawings should be kept simple, to keep the pace lively. Students in the opposing team locate the scene in their books and read it aloud. If they are incorrect, the illustrator's team has a chance to guess. Involve students in setting up a scoring system and any other necessary rules.

11. Play "The Dating Game." Choose three boys in class to be the "bachelors." Give each a card with a male character's name on it. They are not to reveal what is written on the card. Choose one girl to be the "bachelorette." Again, give her a card with a female character's name from the play on it that she will keep to herself. Set them up in the front of the room and have the bachelorette (in character) ask questions of each of the three bachelors, and they must respond in character. The students in the "studio audience" must take notes about what each bachelor and the bachelorette says in an effort to identify their characters. After asking several questions each, allow the "bachelorette" to select one of the "bachelors as a date, giving reasons why she selected him. Also, audience members can then identify who's who in the front of the room. Switch students and cards... do it again. It can also be dome with a "bachelor" selecting from three "bachelorettes."

ELECTRONIC ENRICHMENT WEBQUEST

Much Ado About Nothing WebQuest

Welcome to the *Much Ado About Nothing* WebQuest. You will be placed in four teams: two teams of girls and two teams of boys. Each team will be assigned a particular character from *Much Ado About Nothing* and be given a series of projects relating to that character.

For this series of assignments, you will need to access the World Wide Web (Internet sites have been listed on your assignment sheets for you). Be sure to work together to create your best work! Each group will do the following:

Character Comparisons:
Research a character from another of Shakespeare's works and compare that character's attitudes and behaviors to those of your group's character. Make a poster depicting the situations.

Send in the Clowns:
Research a famous clown from American 20th century and compare him to Dogberry. Make a poster memorializing your group's clown.

Sonnets:
Write a sonnet and write it neatly on a fancy scroll, tied with a bit of ribbon.

Character Journals:
Create a journal for your character that is neither written on lined paper nor word processed. Remember that these did not exist is Shakespeare's day! Incorporate vocabulary words from the unit into your journal entries. Be creative and have a sense of the character's "voice."

Much Ado About Nothing WebQuest
Group 1: Beatrice

Welcome members of Beatrice's group! You will need to collaborate on each of the following to complete your WebQuest

Part I: Character Comparisons:
Read Katherine's final speech in William Shakespeare's *The Taming of the Shrew*. After analyzing the character of Katherine, ask yourself if Beatrice would agree with Katherine's words. Why or why not? Use the links below to help you:
Shakespeare On-Line: http://www-tech.mit.edu/Shakespeare/taming_shrew/full.html
Character Analysis of Katherine http://www.sparknotes.com/shakespeare/shrew/canalysis.html

Part II: Send in the Clowns
Research the 1920's silent film star and clown, Charlie Chaplin. Provide background information as well as a study of his comedic style. How was his style of clowning reflective of the time period in which he lived? Compare Charlie Chaplin to Dogberry in *Much Ado About Nothing*.
Clown Ministry: Charles Chaplin   http://www.clown-ministry.com
Charlie Chaplin Museum   http://www.chaplinmuseum.com/
Charlie Chaplin Archive   http://www.charliechaplinarchive.org

Part III: Sonnets
Hero claims to have found letters and poems written by Beatrice as proof of Beatrice's love for Benedick. Create a sonnet that Beatrice would have written for her true love (be sure to use her "voice"). Be aware that there is more to a sonnet than just the rhyme scheme and the iambic pentameter. Check out the sites below to find out more:
Writing The Sonnet   http://www.writing.upenn.edu/~afilreis/88/sonnet.html
Poetry For Dummies   http://www.dummies.com/WileyCDA/DummiesArticle/id-1748.html
(NOTE: no one is calling anyone a "Dummy"... it's just the name of a very good site!)

Part IV: Character Journals
Create a journal for Beatrice that includes the following entries:
1. Beatrice's early encounters with Benedick (alluded to in Act II) one year prior
2. Beatrice's reaction to the news that Benedick was arriving with Don Pedro
3. Beatrice's reaction to the news about Hero's engagement to Claudio
4. Beatrice's lamentations for the way she treated Benedick after she learns of his feelings for her
5. Beatrice reaction once she learns of the machinations to get her and Benedick together.

Remember that there was no lined paper and no word processors in Shakespeare's day. Create a journal that might have been found in Beatrice's chamber.

Much Ado About Nothing WebQuest
Group 2: Benedick

Welcome members of Benedick's group! You will need to collaborate on each of the following to complete your WebQuest

Part I: Character Comparisons:
Read Romeo's lines regarding his first reaction to the sight of Juliet in William Shakespeare's *Romeo and Juliet*. After analyzing the character of Romeo and his experiences with love, ask yourself if Benedick would agree with how quickly Romeo falls in love. Why or why not? Remind yourself that it only took Benedick overhearing a brief conversation for his whole attitude on love to change! Use the links below to help you:
   Shakespeare On-Line: http://www-tech.mit.edu/Shakespeare/romeo_juliet/full.html
   Character Analysis of Romeo http://www.sparknotes.com/shakespeare/romeojuliet/canalysis.html

Part II: Send in the Clowns
Research the 1950's clown, Red Skelton. Provide background information as well as a study of his comedic style. How was his style of clowning reflective of the time period in which he lived? Compare Red Skelton to Dogberry in *Much Ado About Nothing*.
   Clown Ministry: Red Skelton   http://www.clown-ministry.com
   Red Skelton: A Performance Tribute   http://www.skeltontribute.com/
   Shrine Clowns: Red Skelton   http://www.shrineclowns.com/html/red_skelton.html

Part III: Sonnets
Claudio claims to have found letters and poems written by Benedick as proof of Benedick's love for Beatrice. Create a sonnet that Benedick would have written for his true love (be sure to use his "voice"). Be aware that there is more to a sonnet than just the rhyme scheme and the iambic pentameter. Check out the sites below to find out more:
   Writing The Sonnet   http://www.writing.upenn.edu/~afilreis/88/sonnet.html
   Poetry For Dummies   http://www.dummies.com/WileyCDA/DummiesArticle/id-1748.html
   (NOTE: no one is calling anyone a "Dummy"... it's just the name of a very good site!)

Part IV: Character Journals
Create a journal for Benedick that includes the following entries:
1. Benedick's early encounters with Beatrice (alluded to in Act II) one year prior
2. Benedick's reaction to Beatrice's "welcome" upon his arrival in Messina
3. Benedick's reaction to the news about Claudio's engagement to Hero
4. Benedick's further reactions (besides those in the text) to the news that Beatrice loves him
5. Benedick's reaction once he learns of the machinations to get him and Beatrice together.

Remember that there was no lined paper and no word processors in Shakespeare's day. Create a journal that might have been found in Benedick's satchel.

Much Ado About Nothing WebQuest
Group 3: Hero

Welcome members of Hero's group! You will need to collaborate on each of the following to complete your WebQuest

Part I: Character Comparisons:
    Read Friar Lawrence's plan to help Juliet in William Shakespeare's *Romeo and Juliet*. After analyzing the character of Juliet, ask yourself if Hero would have agreed with Friar Lawrence's plot as readily as she did that of Friar Francis. Why or why not? Compare the two plans and their outcomes. Use the links below to help you:
        Shakespeare On-Line: http://www-tech.mit.edu/Shakespeare/romeo_juliet/full.html
        Character Analysis of Juliet http://www.sparknotes.com/shakespeare/romeojuliet/canalysis.html

Part II: Send in the Clowns
    Research the 1950's clown, Don Knotts. Provide background information as well as a study of his comedic style. How was his style of clowning reflective of the time period in which he lived? Compare Don Knotts to Dogberry in *Much Ado About Nothing*.
        Clown Ministry: Don Knotts   http://www.clown-ministry.com
        The Naked Don Knotts   http://www.interestingideas.com/ii/knotts.htm
        Growing Up With Don Knotts   http://movies.ign.com/articles/691/691696p1.html

Part III: Sonnets
    Create a sonnet that Hero would have written for her true love, Claudio (be sure to use her "voice"). Be aware that there is more to a sonnet than just the rhyme scheme and the iambic pentameter. Check out the sites below to find out more:
        Writing The Sonnet   http://www.writing.upenn.edu/~afilreis/88/sonnet.html
        Poetry For Dummies http://www.dummies.com/WileyCDA/DummiesArticle/id-1748.html
        (NOTE: no one is calling anyone a "Dummy"... it's just the name of a very good site!)

Part IV: Character Journals
    Create a journal for Hero that includes the following entries:
1. Hero's reaction to the first time she saw Claudio
2. Hero's reaction to the news that Don Pedro had wooed her for Claudio
3. Hero's reaction to Don Pedro's plan to bring Beatrice and Benedick together
4. Hero's reactions to Claudio's treatment of her at the church
5. Hero's reaction to learning that she will be marrying Claudio after all

Remember that there was no lined paper and no word processors in Shakespeare's day. Create a journal that might have been found in Hero's bed chamber.

Much Ado About Nothing WebQuest
Group 4: Claudio

Welcome members of Claudio's group! You will need to collaborate on each of the following to complete your WebQuest

Part I: Character Comparisons:
Read Romeo's lines denouncing Juliet as the cause of all his problems after he kills Tybalt in Act III of William Shakespeare's *Romeo and Juliet*. After analyzing the character of Romeo, ask yourself if Claudio would have agreed with Romeo's lamentations. Why or why not? Compare the two young men and their attitudes toward the women they "love" when something goes wrong.. Use the links below to help you:

Shakespeare On-Line: http://www-tech.mit.edu/Shakespeare/romeo_juliet/full.html
Character Analysis of Romeo   http://www.sparknotes.com/shakespeare/romeojuliet/canalysis.html

Part II: Send in the Clowns
Research the 1930's clown, Groucho Marx. Provide background information as well as a study of his comedic style. How was his style of clowning reflective of the time period in which he lived? Compare Groucho Marx to Dogberry in *Much Ado About Nothing*.

Clown Ministry: The Marx Brothers   http://www.clown-ministry.com
The Life and Wisdom of Groucho Marx   http://www.groucho-marx.com/
The Marx Brothers   http://www.marx-brothers.org/

Part III: Sonnets
Create a sonnet that Claudio would have written for Hero (be sure to use his "voice"). Be aware that there is more to a sonnet than just the rhyme scheme and the iambic pentameter. Check out the sites below to find out more:

Writing The Sonnet   http://www.writing.upenn.edu/~afilreis/88/sonnet.html
Poetry For Dummies   http://www.dummies.com/WileyCDA/DummiesArticle/id-1748.html
(NOTE: no one is calling anyone a "Dummy"... it's just the name of a very good site!)

Part IV: Character Journals
Create a journal for Claudio that includes the following entries:
1. Claudio's reaction to the first time he saw Hero
2. Claudio's reaction to the news that Don Pedro had wooed Hero for himself (other than that in the text of the play)
3. Claudio's reactions to having seen "Hero" at the window
4. Claudio's reactions to the news of Hero's "death"
5. Claudio's reaction after learning that he is marrying Hero after all

Remember that there was no lined paper and no word processors in Shakespeare's day. Create a journal that might have been found in Claudio's satchel.

UNIT TESTS

SHORT ANSWER UNIT TEST 1 - *Much Ado About Nothing*

I. Matching/Identify

____ 1. Dogberry   A. seen on at the window with Borachio

____ 2. Benedick   B. claims to speak "all mirth and no matter"

____ 3. Antonio   C. concocts the plot to humiliate Hero

____ 4. Claudio   D. Devises the plan to restore Hero's reputation

____ 5. Hero   E. constable of Messina

____ 6. Borachio   F. is indignant that "beauty is a witch"

____ 7. Verges   G. A "plain dealing villain" who sets out to cause trouble

____ 8. Leonato   H. "cannot endure [the] Lady Tongue"

____ 9. Beatrice   I. the governor's brother

____ 10. Friar Francis J. Borachio's sidekick

____ 11. Don John   K. woos Leonato's daughter for another

____ 12. Balthasar   L. the constable's assistant

____ 13. Don Pedro   M. referred to as a "rotten orange"

____ 14. Conrad   N. the governor of Messina

____ 15. Margaret   O. he sings the songs in the play

SHORT ANSWER UNIT TEST 1 - *Much Ado About Nothing* page 2

II. Short Answer

1. Describe Beatrice's greeting to Benedick upon his arrival.

2. Fully describe what Don Pedro intends to do for Claudio.

3. Describe Don John's true feelings toward his brother, Don Pedro.

4. How does Beatrice further insult Benedick at Leonato's masquerade party?

5. What plan does Don Pedro begin to concoct regarding his friend Signior Benedick?

SHORT ANSWER UNIT TEST 1 - *Much Ado About Nothing* page 3

6. Fully describe the plan Borachio devises that pleases Don John.

7. What "unfavorable" changes in Claudio's behavior does Benedick seem to notice since they arrived in Messina?

8. List three of the qualities a woman must possess before Benedick will even consider her for a wife.

9. What story do Don Pedro, Balthasar, and Claudio tell while Benedick is hiding in the arbor?

10. Explain why Hero claims that she will never tell Beatrice of Benedick's "affections."

SHORT ANSWER UNIT TEST 1 - *Much Ado About Nothing* page 4

11. How does Don John "prove" his accusations about Hero?

12. Who is Dogberry? Describe him.

13. Describe Leonato's reaction to the Count's accusations against his daughter.

14. Describe the plan that the Friar creates regarding Hero.

15. What things does Leonato insist that Claudio do in order to restore his daughter Hero's honor?

SHORT ANSWER UNIT TEST 1 - *Much Ado About Nothing* page 5

III. Essay

Discuss the elements of a Shakespearean Comedy. Be sure to include the plot line as well as the archetypal characters. Draw from *Much Ado About Nothing* for examples.

SHORT ANSWER UNIT TEST 1 - *Much Ado About Nothing* page 6

IV. Vocabulary

Write down the vocabulary words. Go back later and write down the correct definition for each word.

1.

2.

3.

4.

5.

6.

7.

8.

9.

10.

SHORT ANSWER UNIT TEST 1 ANSWER KEY – *Much Ado About Nothing*

I. Matching/Identify:

E	1. Dogberry	A.	seen on at the window with Borachio
H	2. Benedick	B.	claims to speak "all mirth and no matter"
I	3. Antonio	C.	concocts the plot to humiliate Hero
F	4. Claudio	D.	devises the plan to restore Hero's reputation
M	5. Hero	E.	constable of Messina
C	6. Borachio	F.	is indignant that "beauty is a witch"
L	7. Verges	G.	a "plain dealing villain" who sets out to cause trouble
N	8. Leonato	H.	"cannot endure [the] Lady Tongue"
B	9. Beatrice	I.	the governor's brother
D	10. Friar Francis	J.	Borachio's sidekick
G	11. Don John	K.	woos Leonato's daughter for another
O	12. Balthasar	L.	the constable's assistant
K	13. Don Pedro	M.	referred to as a "rotten orange"
J	14. Conrad	N.	the governor of Messina
A	15. Margaret	O.	he sings the songs in the play

II. Short Answer

1. Describe Beatrice's greeting to Benedick upon his arrival.
    Beatrice immediately begins to insult him and he banters back.

2. Fully describe what Don Pedro intends to do for Claudio.
    Since Claudio seems to be too shy to speak to Hero on his own behalf, Don Pedro says that he will, at a masked ball, pretend to be Claudio and woo Hero for him.

3. Describe Don John's true feelings toward his brother, Don Pedro.
    Don John resents his brother. Don John had gone against Don Pedro in a battle and lost, Don Pedro captured Don John and "reconciled" with him.

4. How does Beatrice further insult Benedick at Leonato's masquerade party?
    While dancing with a masked man, and not knowing that he is Benedick, Beatrice begins to talk negatively about Benedick all the more.

5. What plan does Don Pedro begin to concoct regarding his friend Signior Benedick?
    Don Pedro plots to bring Beatrice and Benedick together.

6. Fully describe the plan Borachio devises that pleases Don John.
    Borachio tells Don John that he will "visit" Margaret in the night and manage to get them both near a window where Don John will attempt to "prove" to Claudio that Hero is unfaithful. Don John will make both Don Pedro and Claudio believe that it is Hero at the window with Borachio and not Margaret.

7. What "unfavorable" changes in Claudio's behavior does Benedick seem to notice since they arrived in Messina?
    Benedick notices that instead of war drums and the fife, the valiant soldier Claudio now seems to prefer chamber music. He says that at one time Claudio would have walked ten miles to get a suit of armor, but now he'll spend ten sleepless nights making a new jacket instead. At one time, Claudio spoke plainly and to the point, but now he writes poetry and plays with words.

8. List three of the qualities a woman must possess before Benedick will even consider her for a wife.
    Benedick claims that she must be rich, wise, virtuous, fair, mild, noble, of good discourse, and an excellent musician.

9. What story do Don Pedro, Balthasar, and Claudio tell while Benedick is hiding in the arbor?
    Don Pedro, Balthasar, and Claudio are talking about how much Beatrice is in love with Signior Benedick.

10. Explain why Hero claims that she will never tell Beatrice of Benedick's "affections."
    As part of her ruse to get Beatrice to change her shrewish ways, Hero says that she would never tell Beatrice about Benedick's feelings because, since Beatrice is such a nasty person, she would make fun of poor Signior Benedick's affections toward her.

11. How does Don John "prove" his accusations about Hero?
    Don John says that he, Don Pedro, and Claudio will stand below Hero's window that night to "witness" Hero's behavior. The reader is already aware that the woman at the window will be Margaret, not Hero.

12. Who is Dogberry? Describe him.
    Dogberry is the bumbling Constable of Messina. Both Dogberry and Verges use incorrect diction (malapropisms) when they speak. They confuse such words as "salvation" for "damnation" and "desertless" for "deserving". This adds to the comic relief of the play.

13. Describe Leonato's reaction to the Count's accusations against his daughter.
    Leonato believes the Count and denounces Hero as his daughter. He also wishes her dead.

14. Describe the plan that the Friar creates regarding Hero.
    The Friar tells Leonato to publicly announce that Hero died after being accused, and that he should keep her hidden. The Friar believes that Claudio will feel remorse for his role in her "death" and eventually realize that he had been wrong about her faithfulness. If this does not work, the Friar says that Leonato can put Hero in a cloister.

15. What things does Leonato insist that Claudio do in order to restore his daughter Hero's honor?
    Claudio must: 1) publicly proclaim that he was wrong and Hero was innocent of any wrongdoing, 2) hang an epitaph on her tomb expressing her innocence, and 3) marry a "niece" of Leonato's that looks just like Hero.

Parts III and IV:

For the essay portion, answers will vary. The vocabulary section will depend on which words you select from the list.

SHORT ANSWER UNIT TEST 2 - *Much Ado About Nothing*

I. Matching/Identify

____ 1. Beatrice   A. seen on at the window with Borachio

____ 2. Don John   B. claims to speak "all mirth and no matter"

____ 3. Margaret   C. concocts the plot to humiliate Hero

____ 4. Conrad   D. devises the plan to restore Hero's reputation

____ 5. Friar Francis   E. constable of Messina

____ 6. Verges   F. is indignant that "beauty is a witch"

____ 7. Don Pedro   G. a "plain dealing villain" who sets out to cause trouble

____ 8. Dogberry   H. "cannot endure [the] Lady Tongue"

____ 9. Benedick   I. the governor's brother

____ 10. Claudio   J. Borachio's sidekick

____ 11. Hero   K. woos Leonato's daughter for another

____ 12. Leonato   L. the constable's assistant

____ 13. Balthasar   M. referred to as a "rotten orange"

____ 14. Antonio   N. the governor of Messina

____ 15. Borachio   O. he sings the songs in the play

SHORT ANSWER UNIT TEST 2 - *Much Ado About Nothing* page 2

II. Short Answer

1. According to Leonato, who is fighting a "merry war?

2. What is it that Benedick swears will never happen to him?

3. Where does Claudio say he has spent time before coming to Messina?

4. What does Antonio tell Leonato that he has learned from one of his servants?

5. For what does Beatrice say she is thankful to God every night?

6. How does Don John feed false information to Claudio?

7. What hint does Beatrice drop about the possible reason for her treatment of Benedick?

SHORT ANSWER UNIT TEST 2 - *Much Ado About Nothing* page 3

8. Describe the plan Borachio devises that pleases Don John.

9. What is Benedick's reaction to the tale he overhears while hiding in the arbor?

10. What plan has Hero, Margaret, and Ursula agreed to participate in?

11. What is Beatrice's reaction to what she overhears?

12. What false news does Don John bring to Don Pedro and Claudio?

13. What does Claudio intend to do if he finds out that Hero truly is inappropriately seeing other men?

14. What is Claudio's accusation against Hero?

SHORT ANSWER UNIT TEST 2 - *Much Ado About Nothing* page 4

15. Describe what Claudio does at Hero's tomb.

SHORT ANSWER UNIT TEST 2 - *Much Ado About Nothing* page 5

III. Composition
　　　Describe the various roles of a "clown" or "fool" in comedy. Fully explain how Dogberry fits into this role in *Much Ado About Nothing*.

SHORT ANSWER UNIT TEST 2 - *Much Ado About Nothing* page 6

IV. Vocabulary

    Write down the vocabulary words. Go back later and write down the correct definitions for the words.

1.

2.

3.

4.

5.

6.

7.

8.

9.

10.

ANSWER KEY: SHORT ANSWER UNIT TEST 2 - *Much Ado About Nothing*

I. Matching/Identify

B	1. Beatrice	A. seen on at the window with Borachio
G	2. Don John	B. claims to speak "all mirth and no matter"
A	3. Margaret	C. concocts the plot to humiliate Hero
J	4. Conrad	D. devises the plan to restore Hero's reputation
D	5. Friar Francis	E. constable of Messina
L	6. Verges	F. is indignant that "beauty is a witch"
K	7. Don Pedro	G. a "plain dealing villain" who sets out to cause trouble
E	8. Dogberry	H. "cannot endure [the] Lady Tongue"
H	9. Benedick	I. the governor's brother
F	10. Claudio	J. Borachio's sidekick
M	11. Hero	K. woos Leonato's daughter for another
N	12. Leonato	L. the constable's assistant
O	13. Balthasar	M. referred to as a "rotten orange"
I	14. Antonio	N. the governor of Messina
C	15. Borachio	O. he sings the songs in the play

II. Short Answer

1. According to Leonato, who is fighting a "merry war?"
    Beatrice and Benedick continuously bicker whenever they are in each other's company. This is the "merry war" that Leonato refers to.

2. What is it that Benedick swears will never happen to him?
    Benedick swears that he will never fall in love and marry.

3. Where does Claudio say he has spent time before coming to Messina?
    Claudio has been fighting in a war. Now that the war is over, he is ready to think about love.

4. What does Antonio tell Leonato that he has learned from one of his servants?
    Antonio claims that one of his servants overheard the Don Pedro will woo Leonato's daughter, Hero.

5. For what does Beatrice say she is thankful to God every night?
    She says that she is thankful that she has no husband, and that she does not want to marry.

6. How does Don John feed false information to Claudio?
    Don John tells a masked Claudio – Don John knows it is Claudio even though Claudio claims to be Signior Benedick– that Don Pedro is wooing the fair Hero for himself. This makes Claudio angry because Don Pedro had promised to woo Hero for him.

7. What hint does Beatrice drop about the possible reason for her treatment of Benedick?
    When speaking of Benedick, she admits that he lent his heart to her for a while, but he hurt her.

8. Describe the plan Borachio devises that pleases Don John.
    Borachio tells Don John that he will "visit" Margaret in the night and manage to get them both near a window where Don John will attempt to "prove" to Claudio that Hero is unfaithful. Don John will make both Don Pedro and Claudio believe that it is Hero at the window with Borachio and not Margaret.

9. What is Benedick's reaction to the tale he overhears while hiding in the arbor?
    He is stunned and changes his mind about never marrying. He claims that he will have Beatrice as his wife.

10. What plan has Hero, Margaret, and Ursula agreed to participate in?
    The women know about Don Pedro's plans for Benedick, and they are going to do the same to Beatrice. They know that she is hiding nearby, so they begin a conversation in which they state that Benedick is on love with Beatrice.

11. What is Beatrice's reaction to what she overhears?
    Beatrice feels badly for the way she has acted and she wants Benedick to "love on" because she is about to change her ways.

12. What news does Don John bring to Don Pedro and Claudio?
    Don John claims that Hero is disloyal to Claudio with other men.

13. What does Claudio intend to do if he finds out that Hero truly is inappropriately seeing other men?
    Claudio says that if what Don John says is true, then he will shame Hero publicly at the wedding.

14. What is Claudio's accusation against Hero?
    Claudio claims that Hero is "an approved wanton" and that she has been unfaithful to him with Borachio. He tells those at the wedding that he saw Hero at the window with Borachio the night before.

15. Describe what Claudio does at Hero's tomb.
    Claudio reads a poem that he wrote about Hero, and he hangs it on her tomb.

Parts III and IV:

For the essay portion, answers will vary. The vocabulary section will depend on which words you select from the list.

ADVANCED SHORT ANSWER TEST - *Much Ado About Nothing*

I. Matching/Identify

____ 1. Beatrice.   A. seen on at the window with Borachio

____ 2. Don John   B. claims to speak "all mirth and no matter"

____ 3. Margaret   C. concocts the plot to humiliate Hero

____ 4. Conra   D. devises the plan to restore Hero's reputation

____ 5. Friar Francis   E. constable of Messina

____ 6. Verges   F. is indignant that "beauty is a witch"

____ 7. Don Pedro   G. a "plain dealing villain" who sets out to cause trouble

____ 8. Dogberry   H. "cannot endure [the] Lady Tongue"

____ 9. Benedick   I. the governor's brother

____ 10. Claudio   J. Borachio's sidekick

____ 11. Hero   K. woos Leonato's daughter for another

____ 12. Leonato   L. the constable's assistant

____ 13. Balthasar   M. referred to as a "rotten orange"

____ 14. Antonio   N. the governor of Messina

____ 15. Borachio   O. he sings the songs in the play

ADVANCED SHORT ANSWER TEST - *Much Ado About Nothing* page 2

II. Short Answers

1. Attribute two negative and two positive character traits for each of the following. Be sure to support each trait with specific evidence from the text
    a. Beatrice

    b. Benedick

    c. Claudio

    d. Hero

    e. Leonato

    f. Don Pedro

ADVANCED SHORT ANSWER TEST - *Much Ado About Nothing* page 3

2. Many women in today's society are abused by their significant others. Why do you suppose Hero still wants to marry Claudio even after he treated he so badly at the church? What could her decision to continue to stay with him say about women in general?

3. When Hero is denounced by Claudio in the church, Leonato immediately believes Claudio's accusations and wishes that his daughter was dead. What does this say about his character? What seems to be his biggest concern surrounding the scandal?

4. In *Romeo and Juliet*, it is Friar Lawrence who comes up with the plan to keep the two lovers together. Friar Francis plays a similar role in *Much Ado About Nothing*. Consider what Shakespeare's attitudes might be about the role of the clergy in Elizabethan times.

ADVANCED SHORT ANSWER TEST - *Much Ado About Nothing* page 4

5. Much of the action of *Much Ado About Nothing* is propelled by the fact that certain characters "happen" to overhear what others are saying. Benedick eavesdrops on a conversation between Don Pedro and Claudio. Beatrice "accidentally" overhears what Hero and Margaret say about Benedick's feelings for her. Don John "hears" from an outside "source" that Don Pedro is wooing Hero for himself and share this "truth" with Claudio. What social comments might Shakespeare be making about eavesdropping and rumors? It has been suggested by critics that the play was originally titled *Much Ado About Noting* (as in "noting" what one hears from others). Would this have been a more appropriate title? Explain why or why not.

6. Why do you suppose Beatrice and Benedick were so easily taken in by the plot to bring them together? What does this suggest about the "merry war" between them?

7. Hero is a most obedient daughter who does whatever her father tells her to. What does this say about the role between fathers and daughters in Elizabethan times? How have the relationships between fathers and daughters changed in the time since?

ADVANCED SHORT ANSWER TEST - *Much Ado About Nothing* page 5

8. Examine the relationship between men and women in *Much Ado About Nothing*. What does each relationship (Hero/Claudio, Beatrice/Benedick, and Margaret/Borachio) demonstrate about gender roles in Elizabethan society? Have these gender roles changed in the time since? Give reasons to support your answer.

9. Examine the irony of the fact that marital advice/machination is concocted by a man who has taken a vow to never marry.

10. Note the fact that when Don John tells Claudio that Don Pedro is attempting to woo Hero for himself, Claudio instantly berates Hero in his speeches by saying that "beauty is a witch." Moments later, Don Pedro breaks the news to Claudio that Hero has been won for him, and once again, his attitude toward Hero immediately changes to happiness. What do these instances demonstrate about Claudio's character?

ADVANCED SHORT ANSWER TEST - *Much Ado About Nothing* page 6

III. Composition

    Return each of the following to its proper line format. Then define blank verse and fully describe how it works. Why would Shakespeare decide to use blank verse for many of his speeches?

1. Thou wilt be like a lover presently and tire the hearer with a book of words. If thou dost love fair Hero, cherish it, and I will break with her and with her father, and thou shalt have her. Was't not to this end that thou began'st to twist so fine a story?

2. What need the bridge much broader than the flood? The fairest grant is the necessity. Look, what will serve is fit: 'tis once, thou lovest, and I will fit thee with the remedy. I know we shall have reveling to-night: I will assume thy part in some disguise and tell fair Hero I am Claudio.

ADVANCED SHORT ANSWER TEST - *Much Ado About Nothing* page 7

IV. Vocabulary

A. Listen to the vocabulary words and write them here. Go back and write a definition for each.

1.

2.

3.

4.

5.

6.

7.

8.

9.

10.

11.

12.

    B. For the following topic, include at least five of the vocabulary words in your response.

Describe what performing in a Shakespearean production would have been like, and then describe the changes that Charles II brought to the English stage when he returned from his exile in France.

MULTIPLE CHOICE UNIT TEST 1 - *Much Ado About Nothing*

I. Matching

____ 1.   Dogberry   A. seen on at the window with Borachio

____ 2.   Benedick   B. claims to speak "all mirth and no matter"

____ 3.   Antonio   C. concocts the plot to humiliate Hero

____ 4.   Claudio   D. devises the plan to restore Hero's reputation

____ 5.   Hero   E. constable of Messina

____ 6.   Borachio   F. is indignant that "beauty is a witch"

____ 7.   Verges   G. a "plain dealing villain" who sets out to cause trouble

____ 8.   Leonato   H. "cannot endure [the] Lady Tongue"

____ 9.   Beatrice   I. the governor's brother

____ 10. Friar Francis   J. Borachio's sidekick

____ 11. Don John   K. woos Leonato's daughter for another

____ 12. Balthasar   L. the constable's assistant

____ 13. Don Pedro   M. referred to as a "rotten orange"

____ 14. Conrad   N. the governor of Messina

____ 15. Margaret   O. he sings the songs in the play

MULTIPLE CHOICE UNIT TEST 1 - *Much Ado About Nothing* page 2

II. Multiple Choice

1. Describe Beatrice's greeting to Benedick upon his arrival.
    a. She immediately begins to insult him.
    b. She leaves the room because she cannot bear to look at him.
    c. She rushes into his arms and greets him with a kiss.
    d. She slaps his face for insulting her.

2. What does Don Pedro intend to do for Claudio?
    a. He intends to convince Beatrice to marry Claudio.
    b. He intends to woo Leonato's daughter Hero for the Count Claudio.
    c. He intends to make Claudio a knight of the realm.
    d. He intends to protect Claudio in all upcoming battles

3. What are Don John's true feelings toward his brother, Don Pedro?
    a. He resents Don Pedro.
    b. He is angry that Don Pedro will not allow him to pursue Hero.
    c. He is happy to be reunited with Don Pedro after a long feud.
    d. He wishes to kill his brother.

4. How does Beatrice further insult Benedick at Leonato's masquerade party?
    a. Beatrice, not knowing it is Benedick she is dancing with, talks negatively about him.
    b. Beatrice taunts him publicly at Leonato's party.
    c. Beatrice refuses his proposal of marriage.
    d. Beatrice tells Benedick that it is Hero who is in love with him, not her.

5. What plan does Don Pedro begin to concoct?
    a. He plans to discredit Don John in Leonato's eyes
    b. He plans to ruin the marriage between Claudio and Hero
    c. He plans to bring Beatrice and Benedick together
    d. He plans to kill Leonato and steal Hero away

6. What plan does Borachio devise that pleased Don John?
    a. Borachio will use Margaret to discredit Hero in Claudio's eyes.
    b. Borachio will lure Don Pedro to a place where he can be easily ambushed.
    c. Borachio will foil Don Pedro's attempts to bring Benedick and Beatrice together.
    d. Borachio will woo Hero away from Claudio.

MULTIPLE CHOICE UNIT TEST 1 - *Much Ado About Nothing* page 3

7. Which of the following is not one of the changes in Claudio's behavior that Benedick notices?
    a. He has begun to listen to chamber music.
    b. He has shaved his beard.
    c. He stays up late fashioning new clothes.
    d. He begins to speak and write in poetic form.

8. For what reason must a woman posses specific qualities according to Benedick?
    a. She must posses these qualities in order to get to go to Heaven.
    b. She must posses these qualities to become a true lady.
    c. She must posses these qualities in order to represent her family properly.
    d. She must posses these qualities or he would never consider marrying her.

9. What story do Don Pedro, Balthasar, and Claudio tell while Benedick is hiding in the arbor?
    a. They joke about how Don Pedro wooed Hero for Claudio.
    b. They plot the murder of Leonato.
    c. They talk about how Hero has been unfaithful to Claudio.
    d. They say that Beatrice is in love with Signior Benedick.

10. Why does Hero claim that she will never tell Beatrice of Benedick's "affections?"
    a. Beatrice would only make fun of Benedick's feelings.
    b. Beatrice wouldn't believe her anyway, so why bother?
    c. Beatrice is already in love with Don Pedro.
    d. Beatrice already knows that Benedick is in love with her.

11. How does Don John intend to "prove" his accusations?
    a. He has a letter written by Hero to her lover.
    b. He, Don Pedro, and Claudio will hide below Hero's window and watch what happens.
    c. Beatrice has produced Hero's diary, and in it Hero writes of her visits from Borachio.
    d. He will threaten Hero upon pain of death to confess.

12. Who is Dogberry?
    a. the town constable
    b. Leonato's servant
    c. Beatrice's father
    d. Don John's accomplice

MULTIPLE CHOICE UNIT TEST 1 - *Much Ado About Nothing* page 4

13. Describe Leonato's reaction to the Count's accusations.
    a. Leonato immediately challenges Claudio to a duel.
    b. Leonato takes his daughter away to protect her.
    c. Leonato attacks Claudio.
    d. Leonato denounces Hero and wishes she were dead.

14 What plan does the Friar create regarding Hero?
    a. He plans to give her a potion that will make her appear to be dead, but she will really only be asleep.
    b. He tells Leonato to publicly announce that Hero died after being accused, and that he should keep her hidden. Then Claudio will feel remorse.
    c. He tells Leonato to put her away in a convent to avoid scandal.
    d. He plans to disguise Hero as a man so she can spy on Don John and expose him for the liar he is.

15. Which of the following is not one of the things Leonato insists that Claudio do in order to restore his daughter Hero's honor?
    a. Claudio must sing a dirge at Hero's tomb in her memory.
    b. Claudio must hang an epitaph on Heros tomb proclaiming her innocence.
    c. Claudio must publicly proclaim that he was wrong about Hero.
    d. Claudio must marry a niece who looks exactly like Hero in her place.

MULTIPLE CHOICE UNIT TEST 1 - *Much Ado About Nothing* page 5

III. Composition

1. Attribute two negative and two positive character traits for each of the following. Be sure to support each trait with specific evidence from the text.

    a. Beatrice

    b. Benedick

    c. Claudio

    d. Hero

2. When Claudio was attacking Hero in the church, why do you suppose Beatrice didn't speak up to defend her? Beatrice claims that she and Hero have been sharing a bed for over a year; wouldn't she have noticed if Hero had taken a lover?

MULTIPLE CHOICE UNIT TEST 1 - *Much Ado About Nothing* page 6

3. Does Claudio really love Hero? Give textual evidence to support your answer.

4. Many women in today's society are abused by their significant others. Why do you suppose Hero still wants to marry Claudio even after he treated he so badly at the church? What could her decision to continue to stay with him say about women in general?

5. When Hero is denounced by Claudio in the church, Leonato immediately believes Claudio's accusations and wishes that his daughter was dead. What does this say about his character? What seems to be his biggest concern surrounding the scandal?

MULTIPLE CHOICE UNIT TEST 1 - *Much Ado About Nothing* page 7

6. In Act II, scene i, lines 16-17, Leonato proclaims, "By my troth, niece, thou wilt never get a husband if thou be so shrewd of thy tongue". What is he saying about the roles of women in a relationship? Whose attitude is it that women should not be "so shrewd (clever) of... tongue"? Do men seem to be threatened by strong women? Explain.

7. In *Romeo and Juliet*, it is Friar Lawrence who comes up with the plan to keep the two lovers together. Friar Francis plays a similar role in *Much Ado About Nothing*. Consider what Shakespeare's attitudes might be about the role of the clergy in Elizabethan times.

8. Note that Claudio is not filled with remorse at the news that Hero has died. He only feels regret once Borachio confesses to the plot. Even then, Claudio claims that his only sin was in mistaking Margaret for Hero. What does this show about Claudio's character?

MULTIPLE CHOICE UNIT TEST 1 - *Much Ado About Nothing* page 8

9. Much of the action of *Much Ado About Nothing* is propelled by the fact that certain characters "happen" to overhear what others are saying. Benedick eavesdrops on a conversation between Don Pedro and Claudio. Beatrice "accidentally" overhears what Hero and Margaret say about Benedick's feelings for her. Don John "hears" from an outside "source" that Don Pedro is wooing Hero for himself and share this "truth" with Claudio. What social comments might Shakespeare be making about eavesdropping and rumors? It has been suggested by critics that the play was originally titled *Much Ado About Noting* (as in "noting" what one hears from others). Would this have been a more appropriate title? Explain why or why not.

10. Why do you suppose Hero faints at Claudio's accusation instead of getting angry and stalking out of the church? Would the situation have been different if it had been Benedick who accused Beatrice? Explain.

MULTIPLE CHOICE UNIT TEST 1 - *Much Ado About Nothing* page 9

IV. Vocabulary - Match the correct definitions to the words.

____ 1. victual   A. sharp speech; ill-tempered; nagging

____ 2. betwixt: B. one who changes to the opposite party, reverses principles

____ 3. turncoat   C. a small drum used to accompany oneself on a pipe or fife

____ 4. obstinate   D. those who act without moral restraint; dissolute people

____ 5. mortifying   E. unrestrained or excessive indulgence of sexual desire

____ 6. betroths   F. to fish with hook and line

____ 7. shrewd   G. stone showing curved, colored bands or other markings

____ 8. cuckold   H. food supplies; provisions

____ 9. libertines   I. promises to give in marriage

____ 10. perturbation   J. extremely bad reputation, public reproach

____ 11. tabor   K. in a middle; between

____ 12. reprove   L. to urge on; stimulate or prompt to action

____ 13. angling   M. firmly or stubbornly adhering to one's purpose, opinion

____ 14. agate   N. a sudden feeling of apprehensive uneasiness

____ 15. incite   O. to criticize or correct

____ 16. defiled   P. painfully difficult or burdensome work; toil

____ 17. lechery   Q. the husband of an unfaithful wife

____ 18. qualm   R. made filthy or dirty; unclean

____ 19. travail   S. mental disquiet, disturbance, or agitation

____ 20. infamy   T. humiliating or shameful, injurious to one's pride or self-respect

MULTIPLE CHOICE UNIT TEST 2 - *Much Ado About Nothing*

I. Matching

____ 1. Beatrice.   A. seen on at the window with Borachio

____ 2. Don John   B. claims to speak "all mirth and no matter"

____ 3. Margaret   C. concocts the plot to humiliate Hero

____ 4. Conrad   D. devises the plan to restore Hero's reputation

____ 5. Friar Francis   E. constable of Messina

____ 6. Verges   F. is indignant that "beauty is a witch"

____ 7. Don Pedro   G. a "plain dealing villain" who sets out to cause trouble

____ 8. Dogberry   H. "cannot endure [the] Lady Tongue"

____ 9. Benedick   I. the governor's brother

____ 10. Claudio   J. Borachio's sidekick

____ 11. Hero   K. woos Leonato's daughter for another

____ 12. Leonato   L. the constable's assistant

____ 13. Balthasar   M. referred to as a "rotten orange"

____ 14. Antonio   N. the governor of Messina

____ 15. Borachio   O. he sings the songs in the play

MULTIPLE CHOICE UNIT TEST 2 - *Much Ado About Nothing* page 2

II. Multiple Choice

1. According to Leonato, who is fighting a "merry war?"
    a. Don Pedro and Don John
    b. Count Claudio and Hero
    c. Leonato and Antonio
    d. Beatrice and Benedick

2. What is it that Benedick swears will never happen to him?
    a. He swears that he will never be defeated in battle.
    b. He swears that he will never return to Messina after he leaves.
    c. He swears that he will never fall in love and marry.
    d. He swears that he will never allow himself to be insulted by a woman again.

3. Where does Claudio say he has spent time before coming to Messina?
    a. He has been traveling the world seeking the perfect bride.
    b. He has been at a university in a far away land.
    c. He has been at war.
    d. This is the first time he has ever left his home in Aragorn

4. What does Antonio claim to have learned from one of his servants?
    a. Antonio claims that Don Pedro intends to kill Claudio.
    b. Antonio claims that Benedick is in love with Beatrice.
    c. Antonio claims that Don Pedro intends to woo Leonato's daughter.
    d. Antonio claims that Hero has become engaged to Claudio.

5. For what does Beatrice say she is thankful to God every night?
    a. her good health
    b. her chastity
    c. that she is not married
    d. her wit

6. Who does Claudio become angry with after Don John shares what he has "heard?"
    a. Hero
    b. Don John
    c. Don Pedro
    d. Beatrice

7. What news does Don Pedro bring to Claudio?
    a. Don Pedro tells Claudio that Hero has refused to marry him.
    b. Don Pedro tells Claudio that he has won Hero's hand in marriage to Claudio.
    c. Don Pedro tells Claudio that Leonato has refused Claudio's suit.
    d. Don Pedro tells Claudion that Leonato has agreed to the match between Claudio and Hero.

MULTIPLE CHOICE UNIT TEST 2 - *Much Ado About Nothing* page 3

8. What plan does Borachio devise that pleased Don John?
    a. Borachio will use Margaret to discredit Hero in Claudio's eyes.
    b. Borachio will lure Don Pedro to a place where he can be easily ambushed.
    c. Borachio will foil Don Pedro's attempts to bring Benedick and Beatrice together.
    d. Borachio will woo Hero away from Claudio.

9. What is Benedick's reaction to the news he overhears?
    a. He is shocked that Hero is in love with him; he thinks she is too young.
    b. He is shocked that Beatrice loves him, and he says that he loves her as well.
    c. He is angry that Don John would plot against him.
    d. He is insulted that Leonato would assume that he would marry Beatrice.

10. What plan has Hero, Margaret, and Ursula agreed to participate in?
    a. Don John's plot to discredit Don Pedro
    b. Don Pedro's plot to bring Beatrice and Benedick together
    c. Claudio's plan to elope with Hero
    d. Beatrice's plan to entice Benedick to be her husband

11. What is Beatrice's reaction to what she overhears?
    a. She is angry at Benedick for mocking her.
    b. She feels bad for the way she has acted and wants Benedick to "love on" because she is about to change her ways.
    c. She is confused because she is already promised to Don Pedro, but she loves Benedick.
    d. She bursts into tears and says she can never face Benedick again.

12. What false news does Don John bring to Don Pedro and Claudio?
    a. He says that Leonato has suddenly taken ill.
    b. He says that Hero has run away with Conrad.
    c. He says that Hero is unfaithful to Claudio.
    d. He says that Hero has suddenly taken ill.

13. What does Claudio intend to do if he finds out that Hero truly is inappropriately seeing other men?
    a. Claudio intends to kill man who comes to see Hero.
    b. Claudio intends to kill Hero and her lover.
    c. Claudio intends to leave Messina immediately.
    d. Claudio intends to shame Hero publicly at the wedding.

14. What is Claudio's accusation against Hero?
    a. Claudio accuses her of being unfaithful to him with Borachio.
    b. Claudio accuses her of lying to her father about Beatrice and Benedick.
    c. Claudio accuses her of plotting with Don John to marry Benedick.
    d. Claudio accuses her of conspiring against him to win favor with Benedick.

MULTIPLE CHOICE UNIT TEST 2 - *Much Ado About Nothing* page 4

15. What does Claudio do at Hero's tomb?
    a. Claudio sings a song of lament.
    b. Claudio places flowers on her grave and weeps openly.
    c. Claudio reads an epitaph he wrote to Hero.
    d. Claudio enters Hero's tomb to commit suicide, to be with her forever.

MULTIPLE CHOICE UNIT TEST 2 - *Much Ado About Nothing* page 5

III. Composition

1. Examine the relationship between Don Pedro and Don John. To what might you be able to contribute the animosity between them?

2. When Beatrice claims that she "knows [Benedick] of old," what does this suggest about the animosity between them?

3. Why do you suppose Beatrice and Benedick were so easily taken in by the plot to bring them together? What does this suggest about the "merry war" between them?

4. Hero is a most obedient daughter who does whatever her father tells her to. What does this say about the role between fathers and daughters in Elizabethan times? How have the relationships between fathers and daughters changed in the time since?

MULTIPLE CHOICE UNIT TEST 2 - *Much Ado About Nothing* page 6

5. Examine the relationship between men and women in *Much Ado About Nothing*. What does each relationship (Hero/Claudio, Beatrice/Benedick, and Margaret/Borachio) demonstrate about gender roles in Elizabethan society? Have these gender roles changed in the time since? Give reasons to support your answer.

6. Examine the irony of the fact that marital advice/machination is concocted by a man who has taken a vow to never marry.

7. Note the fact that when Don John tells Claudio that Don Pedro is attempting to woo Hero for himself, Claudio instantly berates Hero in his speeches by saying that "beauty is a witch." Moments later, Don Pedro breaks the news to Claudio that Hero has been won for him, and once again, his attitude toward Hero immediately changes to happiness. What do these instances demonstrate about Claudio's character?

8. Suppose Claudio had not been remorseful after hearing Borachio's confession. What would have become of Hero? How might she feel about the situation?

MULTIPLE CHOICE UNIT TEST 2 - *Much Ado About Nothing* page 7

9. Why do you suppose Hero faints at Claudio's accusation instead of getting angry and talking out of the church? Would the situation have been different if it had been Benedick who accused Beatrice? Explain.

10. Suppose that Hero pretended to go along with the Friar's plot and then, when all was to "be set right" between Hero and Claudio at the church, she denounced him for the idiot he is, slapped him in the face and left him at the altar with his mouth hanging open. How might the other characters react? Who might be on Hero's side? Who would take Claudio's side? Explain

MULTIPLE CHOICE UNIT TEST 2 - *Much Ado About Nothing* page 8

IV. Vocabulary - Match the correct definitions to the words.

____ 1. league   A. showing contempt for; scorn

____ 2. flouting   B. misled by means of a petty trick or fraud; deceived

____ 3. liege   C. to cause to be or to become

____ 4. accordant   D. following as a consequence or result

____ 5. enfranchised   E. a close-fitting jacket worn by men in the Renaissance

____ 6. tartly   F. a loud uproar, as from a crowd of people

____ 7. poniards   G. boring, tiring, monotonous, dull

____ 8. cozened   H. feudal lord entitled to allegiance and service

____ 9. orthography   I. sharp in character, spirit, or expression; cutting; caustic

____ 10. ensuing   J. questioning or examining closely or methodically

____ 11. thwarting   K. one who gives a false or misleading appearance

____ 12. doublet   L. the art of writing

____ 13. tedious   M. agreeing; conforming; harmonious

____ 14. catechizing   N. the willful giving of false testimony under oath

____ 15. perjury   O. freed, as from bondage

____ 16. havoc   P. boldness or determination in facing great danger

____ 17. render   Q. great destruction or devastation; ruinous damage

____ 18. dissembler   R. daggers having slender square or triangular blades

____ 19. valor   S. a unit of distance equal to 3.0 statute miles

____ 20. clamor   T. opposing/defeating the efforts, plans, or ambitions of

ANSWER SHEET - *Much Ado About Nothing*
Multiple Choice Unit Tests

I. Matching

1. ___
2. ___
3. ___
4. ___
5. ___
6. ___
7. ___
8. ___
9. ___
10. ___
11. ___
12. ___
13. ___
14. ___
15. ___

II. Multiple Choice

1. ___
2. ___
3. ___
4. ___
5. ___
6. ___
7. ___
8. ___
9. ___
10. ___
11. ___
12. ___
13. ___
14. ___
15. ___

IV. Vocabulary

1. ___
2. ___
3. ___
4. ___
5. ___
6. ___
7. ___
8. ___
9. ___
10. ___
11. ___
12. ___
13. ___
14. ___
15. ___
16. ___
17. ___
18. ___
19. ___
20. ___

ANSWER KEY - *Much Ado About Nothing*
Multiple Choice Unit Test 1

I. Matching	II. Multiple Choice	IV. Vocabulary
1. E	1. A	1. H
2. H	2. B	2. K
3. I	3. A	3. B
4. F	4. A	4. M
5. M	5. B	5. T
6. C	6. A	6. I
7. L	7. B	7. A
8. N	8. D	8. Q
9. B	9. D	9. D
10. D	10. A	10. S
11. G	11. B	11. C
12. O	12. A	12. O
13. K	13. D	13. F
14. J	14. B	14. G
15. A	15. A	15. L
		16. R
		17. E
		18. N
		19. P
		20. J

Answers for Part III will vary.

ANSWER KEY - *Much Ado About Nothing*
Multiple Choice Unit Test 2

I. Matching	II. Multiple Choice	IV. Vocabulary
1. B	1. D	1. S
2. G	2. C	2. A
3. A	3. C	3. H
4. J	4. C	4. M
5. D	5. C	5. O
6. L	6. A	6. I
7. K	7. D	7. R
8. E	8. A	8. B
9. H	9. B	9. L
10. F	10. B	10. D
11. M	11. B	11. T
12. N	12. C	12. E
13. O	13. D	13. G
14. I	14. A	14. J
15. C	15. C	15. N
		16. Q
		17. C
		18. K
		19. P
		20. F

Answers for Part II will vary.

UNIT RESOURCE MATERIALS

BULLETIN BOARD IDEAS - *Much Ado About Nothing*

1. Save one corner of the board for the best of students' Much Ado About Nothing writing assignments.

2. Take one of the word search puzzles from the extra activities packet and with a marker copy it over in a large size on the bulletin board. Write the clue words to find to one side. Invite students prior to and after class to find the words and circle them on the bulletin board.

3. Write several of the most significant quotations from the book onto the board on brightly colored paper.

4. Make a bulletin board listing the vocabulary words for this unit. As you complete sections of the play and discuss the vocabulary for each section, write the definitions on the bulletin board. (If your board is one students face frequently, it will help them learn the words.)

5. Create a visual representation of the Globe Theatre, complete with labeling each part of the theatre.

6.. Devote a bulletin board to Shakespeare's other works, breaking them into the categories of Tragedy, Comedy, and History.

7. Display every day life in Elizabethan England, complete with class distinctions.

8. Sketch costumes for the various characters and display them on a bulletin board with explanations of why each costume was chosen for a particular character.

9. Make a cast list of modern actors in the roles of the characters in *Much Ado About Nothing* (no fair using the cast list from the Kenneth Branaugh film!) and create a movie poster for it.

10. Devote a bulletin board to modern clowns and the roles they play in society. Connect to some of Shakespeare's famous clown characters.

11. Devote a bulletin board to Shakespeare's sonnets, making sure to include the format for creating a Shakespearean sonnet.

12. Create a bulletin board that represents the changes to the English theatre brought about by Charles II after his return from exile in France.

EXTRA ACTIVITIES - *Much Ado About Nothing*

One of the difficulties in teaching a novel is that all students don't read at the same speed. One student who likes to read may take the book home and finish it in a day or two. Sometimes a few students finish the in-class assignments early. The problem, then, is finding suitable extra activities for students.

One thing that seems to help is to keep a little library in the classroom. For this unit on *Much Ado About Nothing,* you might check out from the school library other comedies by William Shakespeare such as *All's Well That Ends Well, Twelfth Night, A Midsummer Night's Dream, Comedy of Errors, Two Gentlemen of Verona,* or *The Merry Wives of Windsor.* Students could then react to whether or not Shakespeare kept to his comic pattern of "Boy Meets Girl, Boy Loses Girl, Boy Gets Girl." Any stories or articles about William Shakespeare (and other playwrights of the time), Charles II, the Globe Theatre (and other Elizabethan theatres) or life in Elizabethan England would also be of interest.

Other things you may keep on hand are puzzles. This manual contains some relating directly to *Much Ado About Nothing* for you. Feel free to duplicate them for your students to use.

Some students may like to draw. You might devise a contest or allow some extra-credit grade for students who draw characters or scenes from *Much Ado About Nothing*. Note, too, that if the students do not want to keep their drawings you may pick up some extra bulletin board materials this way. If you have a contest and you supply the prize (a CD or something like that perhaps), you could, possibly, make the drawing itself a non-returnable entry fee.

The pages which follow contain games, puzzles and worksheets. The keys, when appropriate, immediately follow the puzzle or worksheet. There are two main groups of activities: one group for the unit; that is, generally relating to *Much Ado About Nothing* text, and another group of activities related strictly to *Much Ado About Nothing* vocabulary.

Directions for these games, puzzles and worksheets are self-explanatory. The object here is to provide you with extra materials you may use in any way you choose.

MORE ACTIVITIES - *Much Ado About Nothing*

1. Have students work together to make a time line chronology of the events in the story. Take a large piece of construction paper and on one wall (or however you can physically arrange it in your room) and make the events of the story along it. Students may want to add drawings or cut-out pictures to represent the events (as well as a written statement).

2. Have students design a book cover (front and back and inside flaps) for *Much Ado About Nothing*.

3. Have students design a bulletin board (ready to be put up; not just sketched) for *Much Ado About Nothing*.

4. Have students design a Broadway poster for *Much Ado About Nothing*.

5. Have students design a playbill (front and back and inside flaps) for *Much Ado About Nothing*.

6. From two or more film versions of *Much Ado About Nothing*, play the same scene as depicted by the different directors. Have students analyze the use of lighting, costumes, music, sets, make-up, and characterization. Decide which seems to be truer to Shakespeare's intent and explain why.

7. Select another film version of one of Shakespeare's comedies and analyze it for the director's use of comic elements.

8. In conjunction with the non-fiction assignment, have an Elizabethan Day. Hold a banquet of Elizabethan food & drink, have students dress in Elizabethan costume, and discuss the politics of the period.

Much Ado About Nothing Word List

No.	Word	Clue/Definition
1.	ANTONIO	Governor's brother; uncle to Hero and Beatrice
2.	AVON	Shakespeare's home: Stratford-Upon-___
3.	BALTHASAR	He sings the songs in the play.
4.	BEATRICE	She and Benedick have a love-hate relationship.
5.	BENEDICK	He is tricked into thinking Beatrice loves him.
6.	BLANK	Unrhymed iambic pentameter: ___ verse
7.	BORACHIO	He visits Margaret in the night to deceive Claudio.
8.	CLAUDIO	He was to marry Hero.
9.	COMIC	This kind of relief breaks the emotional tension of a play.
10.	CONRAD	Borachio's sidekick
11.	DENOUNCES	Upon hearing the accusations, Leonato ___ Hero as his daughter.
12.	DIED	The Friar tells Leonato to publicly announce that Hero ___ after being accused.
13.	DOGBERRY	Constable of Messina
14.	DUCATS	Don John gave Borachio 1,000 of these for his part in the scheme.
15.	DUEL	Leonato challenges Claudio to one.
16.	FAINTS	What Hero does after denying Claudio's accusations
17.	FRIAR	He devises the plan to restore Hero's reputation.
18.	HERO	She is disgraced at the altar.
19.	HUSBAND	Beatrice says she is thankful to God every night that she doesn't have one.
20.	INSULTS	Beatrice hurls these at Benedick upon his arrival.
21.	JOHN	Don Pedro's villainous brother
22.	KILL	Beatrice wants Benedick to do this to Claudio for what he did to Hero.
23.	LAMENT	Sad song of regret, usually for a lost love
24.	LEONATO	Governor of Messina
25.	LOVE	Now that the war is over, Claudio is ready to think about this.
26.	MARGARET	She is seen at the window with Borachio.
27.	MARRY	Benedick swears he will never do this, but he later changes his mind.
28.	MESSINA	Setting of Much Ado
29.	ORANGE	Claudio calls Hero a rotten ___.
30.	PARTY	Leonato hosts a masquerade ___ at which the confusion in the play begins.
31.	PEDRO	Woos Leonato's daughter for another: Don ___
32.	SONNET	14 lined poem following ababcdcdefergg pattern
33.	TOOTHACHE	Benedick blames his melancholy behavior on this.
34.	VERGES	Constable's assistant
35.	WIFE	Benedick thinks a good ___ would be rich, wise, virtuous, fair, mild, noble, etc.
36.	WOO	Court with the intent to marry

WORD SEARCH Much Ado About Nothing

```
T L O V E Z M V T I C W W A D C O M I C
E O F W L G A E K N L O I D V U C B F G
R H O Q D Q R R Y S A O F N U O C D H F
A S Z T S N R G T U U W E S K E N A J P
G D D L H X Y E L L D D D C O K L G T H
R X N N C A N S Q T I Z I C J N O S Y S
A P A R T Y C T B S O D Z C K I N C S J
M Q Y W R Q C H P Z E P F D H Q P E H D
N Q L M F S S Z E N L S K C Y W O S T B
T S Z O T K O R E J R S A Z B I S E Q R
L C T R M T W B V F H R F J N Q D C D G
S C O A A E N X N D O L S O J N R N O C
H Q D N A B S U H B E A T R I C E U G X
K S O G R F M S W X L N T N X S L O B Q
L E V E V A G Z I D A A J Z P R B N E P
L A W L K B D D T N I H N O R H G E R F
D S M F A I N T S M A E Q K H P E D R O
F R C E X N L W Q Y M R D H W N F I Y S
X M R H N J K L Q R J O J H M C A P Y W
M B R V B T Z B A L T H A S A R W X D T
```

ANTONIO	COMIC	FRIAR	LOVE	TOOTHACHE
AVON	CONRAD	HERO	MARGARET	VERGES
BALTHASAR	DENOUNCES	HUSBAND	MARRY	WIFE
BEATRICE	DIED	INSULTS	MESSINA	WOO
BENEDICK	DOGBERRY	JOHN	ORANGE	
BLANK	DUCATS	KILL	PARTY	
BORACHIO	DUEL	LAMENT	PEDRO	
CLAUDIO	FAINTS	LEONATO	SONNET	

WORD SEARCH ANSWER KEY Much Ado About Nothing

ANTONIO	COMIC	FRIAR	LOVE	TOOTHACHE
AVON	CONRAD	HERO	MARGARET	VERGES
BALTHASAR	DENOUNCES	HUSBAND	MARRY	WIFE
BEATRICE	DIED	INSULTS	MESSINA	WOO
BENEDICK	DOGBERRY	JOHN	ORANGE	
BLANK	DUCATS	KILL	PARTY	
BORACHIO	DUEL	LAMENT	PEDRO	
CLAUDIO	FAINTS	LEONATO	SONNET	

CROSSWORD Much Ado About Nothing

Across
1. Unrhymed iambic pentameter: ___ verse
5. Beatrice hurls these at Benedick upon his arrival.
8. The Friar tells Leonato to publicly announce that Hero ____ after being accused.
10. He sings the songs in the play.
12. She is disgraced at the altar.
14. This kind of relief breaks the emotional tension of a play.
16. He visits Margaret in the night to deceive Claudio.
17. He is tricked into thinking Beatrice loves him.
19. Governor's brother; uncle to Hero and Beatrice
20. He devises the plan to restore Hero's reputation.
21. Claudio calls Hero a rotten ____.
22. What Hero does after denying Claudio's accusations.

Down
2. Sad song of regret, usually for a lost love
3. Beatrice wants Benedick to do this to Claudio for what he did to Hero.
4. Leonato challenges Claudio to one.
6. Benedick blames his melancholy behavior on this.
7. Borachio's sidekick
9. Benedick swears he will never do this, but he later changes his mind.
11. Governor of Messina
13. Now that the war is over, Claudio is ready to think about this.
15. Don Pedro's villainous brother
18. Don John gave Borachio 1,000 of these for his part in the scheme.
19. Shakespeare's home: Stratford-Upon-___

CROSSWORD ANSWER KEY Much Ado About Nothing

		1 B	2 L	A	3 N	K		4 D				
			A		5 I	N	S	U	L	6 T	S	
			M		L			E		O		7 C
		8 D	I	E	D			L		O		O
			N			9 M		T		N		
	10 B	11 A	L	T	H	A	S	A	R	12 H	E	R	O
		E				R		13 L		A		A
		14 C	O	M	I	C		R	O	C	H	D
	15 J		N					Y		V		H
16 B	O	R	A	C	H	I	O		17 B	E	N	E	18 D	I	C	K
	H		T									U
19 A	N	T	O	N	I	O						C
V							20 F	R	I	A	R
21 O	R	A	N	G	E						T
N						22 F	A	I	N	T	S

Across
1. Unrhymed iambic pentameter: ___ verse
5. Beatrice hurls these at Benedick upon his arrival.
8. The Friar tells Leonato to publicly announce that Hero ____ after being accused.
10. He sings the songs in the play.
12. She is disgraced at the altar.
14. This kind of relief breaks the emotional tension of a play.
16. He visits Margaret in the night to deceive Claudio.
17. He is tricked into thinking Beatrice loves him.
19. Governor's brother; uncle to Hero and Beatrice
20. He devises the plan to restore Hero's reputation.
21. Claudio calls Hero a rotten ____.
22. What Hero does after denying Claudio's accusations.

Down
2. Sad song of regret, usually for a lost love
3. Beatrice wants Benedick to do this to Claudio for what he did to Hero.
4. Leonato challenges Claudio to one.
6. Benedick blames his melancholy behavior on this.
7. Borachio's sidekick
9. Benedick swears he will never do this, but he later changes his mind.
11. Governor of Messina
13. Now that the war is over, Claudio is ready to think about this.
15. Don Pedro's villainous brother
18. Don John gave Borachio 1,000 of these for his part in the scheme.
19. Shakespeare's home: Stratford-Upon-___

MATCHING 1 Much Ado About Nothing

___ 1. BEATRICE   A. Beatrice hurls these at Benedick upon his arrival.

___ 2. CONRAD   B. She and Benedick have a love-hate relationship.

___ 3. CLAUDIO   C. Beatrice says she is thankful to God every night that she doesn't have one.

___ 4. DUCATS   D. Leonato challenges Claudio to one.

___ 5. MESSINA   E. Benedick swears he will never do this, but he later changes his mind.

___ 6. SONNET   F. Don Pedro's villainous brother

___ 7. LEONATO   G. Shakespeare's home: Stratford-Upon-___

___ 8. TOOTHACHE   H. Unrhymed iambic pentameter: ___ verse

___ 9. BLANK   I. This kind of relief breaks the emotional tension of a play.

___10. DOGBERRY   J. Governor of Messina

___11. HUSBAND   K. Governor's brother; uncle to Hero and Beatrice

___12. COMIC   L. He devises the plan to restore Hero's reputation.

___13. DUEL   M. She is disgraced at the altar.

___14. BENEDICK   N. Constable of Messina

___15. MARRY   O. Setting of Much Ado

___16. HERO   P. Claudio calls Hero a rotten ____.

___17. INSULTS   Q. He is tricked into thinking Beatrice loves him.

___18. PEDRO   R. 14 lined poem following ababcdcdefergg pattern

___19. AVON   S. Woos Leonato's daughter for another: Don ___

___20. LAMENT   T. Sad song of regret, usually for a lost love

___21. ORANGE   U. Benedick blames his melancholy behavior on this.

___22. ANTONIO   V. What Hero does after denying Claudio's accusations

___23. FAINTS   W. Don John gave Borachio 1,000 of these for his part in the scheme.

___24. JOHN   X. Borachio's sidekick

___25. FRIAR   Y. He was to marry Hero.

MATCHING 1 ANSWER KEY Much Ado About Nothing

B - 1.	BEATRICE	A. Beatrice hurls these at Benedick upon his arrival.
X - 2.	CONRAD	B. She and Benedick have a love-hate relationship.
Y - 3.	CLAUDIO	C. Beatrice says she is thankful to God every night that she doesn't have one.
W 4.	DUCATS	D. Leonato challenges Claudio to one.
O - 5.	MESSINA	E. Benedick swears he will never do this, but he later changes his mind.
R - 6.	SONNET	F. Don Pedro's villainous brother
J - 7.	LEONATO	G. Shakespeare's home: Stratford-Upon-___
U - 8.	TOOTHACHE	H. Unrhymed iambic pentameter: ___ verse
H - 9.	BLANK	I. This kind of relief breaks the emotional tension of a play.
N -10.	DOGBERRY	J. Governor of Messina
C -11.	HUSBAND	K. Governor's brother; uncle to Hero and Beatrice
I - 12.	COMIC	L. He devises the plan to restore Hero's reputation.
D -13.	DUEL	M. She is disgraced at the altar.
Q -14.	BENEDICK	N. Constable of Messina
E -15.	MARRY	O. Setting of Much Ado
M ·16.	HERO	P. Claudio calls Hero a rotten ____.
A -17.	INSULTS	Q. He is tricked into thinking Beatrice loves him.
S -18.	PEDRO	R. 14 lined poem following ababcdcdefergg pattern
G -19.	AVON	S. Woos Leonato's daughter for another: Don ___
T -20.	LAMENT	T. Sad song of regret, usually for a lost love
P -21.	ORANGE	U. Benedick blames his melancholy behavior on this.
K -22.	ANTONIO	V. What Hero does after denying Claudio's accusations
V -23.	FAINTS	W. Don John gave Borachio 1,000 of these for his part in the scheme.
F -24.	JOHN	X. Borachio's sidekick
L -25.	FRIAR	Y. He was to marry Hero.

MATCHING 2 Much Ado About Nothing

___ 1. PARTY   A. Court with the intent to marry
___ 2. WOO   B. Claudio calls Hero a rotten ____.
___ 3. DIED   C. Unrhymed iambic pentameter: ___ verse
___ 4. COMIC   D. Leonato hosts a masquerade ____ at which the confusion in the play begins.
___ 5. KILL   E. Don John gave Borachio 1,000 of these for his part in the scheme.
___ 6. LEONATO   F. She is seen at the window with Borachio.
___ 7. FAINTS   G. Benedick thinks a good ____ would be rich, wise, virtuous, fair, mild, noble, etc.
___ 8. HERO   H. This kind of relief breaks the emotional tension of a play.
___ 9. DOGBERRY   I. Constable of Messina
___ 10. MARRY   J. Don Pedro's villainous brother
___ 11. JOHN   K. She is disgraced at the altar.
___ 12. VERGES   L. Beatrice hurls these at Benedick upon his arrival.
___ 13. FRIAR   M. Shakespeare's home: Stratford-Upon-___
___ 14. MESSINA   N. Benedick swears he will never do this, but he later changes his mind.
___ 15. INSULTS   O. He visits Margaret in the night to deceive Claudio.
___ 16. ORANGE   P. Governor of Messina
___ 17. PEDRO   Q. Constable's assistant
___ 18. ANTONIO   R. He devises the plan to restore Hero's reputation.
___ 19. DUCATS   S. Governor's brother; uncle to Hero and Beatrice
___ 20. AVON   T. Woos Leonato's daughter for another: Don ___
___ 21. BLANK   U. Sad song of regret, usually for a lost love
___ 22. MARGARET   V. Beatrice wants Benedick to do this to Claudio for what he did to Hero.
___ 23. WIFE   W. The Friar tells Leonato to publicly announce that Hero ____ after being accused.
___ 24. LAMENT   X. What Hero does after denying Claudio's accusations
___ 25. BORACHIO   Y. Setting of Much Ado

MATCHING 2 ANSWER KEY Much Ado About Nothing

D - 1. PARTY
A - 2. WOO
W - 3. DIED
H - 4. COMIC
V - 5. KILL
P - 6. LEONATO
X - 7. FAINTS
K - 8. HERO
I - 9. DOGBERRY
N - 10. MARRY
J - 11. JOHN
Q - 12. VERGES
R - 13. FRIAR
Y - 14. MESSINA
L - 15. INSULTS
B - 16. ORANGE
T - 17. PEDRO
S - 18. ANTONIO
E - 19. DUCATS
M - 20. AVON
C - 21. BLANK
F - 22. MARGARET
G - 23. WIFE
U - 24. LAMENT
O - 25. BORACHIO

A. Court with the intent to marry
B. Claudio calls Hero a rotten ____.
C. Unrhymed iambic pentameter: ____ verse
D. Leonato hosts a masquerade ____ at which the confusion in the play begins.
E. Don John gave Borachio 1,000 of these for his part in the scheme.
F. She is seen at the window with Borachio.
G. Benedick thinks a good ____ would be rich, wise, virtuous, fair, mild, noble, etc.
H. This kind of relief breaks the emotional tension of a play.
I. Constable of Messina
J. Don Pedro's villainous brother
K. She is disgraced at the altar.
L. Beatrice hurls these at Benedick upon his arrival.
M. Shakespeare's home: Stratford-Upon-____
N. Benedick swears he will never do this, but he later changes his mind.
O. He visits Margaret in the night to deceive Claudio.
P. Governor of Messina
Q. Constable's assistant
R. He devises the plan to restore Hero's reputation.
S. Governor's brother; uncle to Hero and Beatrice
T. Woos Leonato's daughter for another: Don ____
U. Sad song of regret, usually for a lost love
V. Beatrice wants Benedick to do this to Claudio for what he did to Hero.
W. The Friar tells Leonato to publicly announce that Hero ____ after being accused.
X. What Hero does after denying Claudio's accusations
Y. Setting of Much Ado

JUGGLE LETTER 1 Much Ado About Nothing

1. VELO   = 1. _____
   Now that the war is over, Claudio is ready to think about this.

2. NSAUBHD   = 2. _____
   Beatrice says she is thankful to God every night that she doesn't have one.

3. KBANL   = 3. _____
   Unrhymed iambic pentameter: ___ verse

4. EIDD   = 4. _____
   The Friar tells Leonato to publicly announce that Hero ____ after being accused.

5. OOENTAL   = 5. _____
   Governor of Messina

6. RBOIAOCH = 6. _____
   He visits Margaret in the night to deceive Claudio.

7. ONTNES   = 7. _____
   14 lined poem following ababcdcdefergg pattern

8. SDEOUNNEC = 8. _____
   Upon hearing the accusations, Leonato ___ Hero as his daughter.

9. IMASENS   = 9. _____
   Setting of Much Ado

10. WOO   =10. _____
    Court with the intent to marry

11. OHNJ   =11. _____
    Don Pedro's villainous brother

12. NCEKBIED =12. _____
    He is tricked into thinking Beatrice loves him.

13. ETCHAHOTO =13. _____
    Benedick blames his melancholy behavior on this.

14. ULED   =14. _____
    Leonato challenges Claudio to one.

15. RGDBEOYR =15. _____
    Constable of Messina

JUGGLE LETTER 1 ANSWER KEY Much Ado About Nothing

1. VELO = 1. LOVE

   Now that the war is over, Claudio is ready to think about this.

2. NSAUBHD = 2. HUSBAND

   Beatrice says she is thankful to God every night that she doesn't have one.

3. KBANL = 3. BLANK

   Unrhymed iambic pentameter: ___ verse

4. EIDD = 4. DIED

   The Friar tells Leonato to publicly announce that Hero ____ after being accused.

5. OOENTAL = 5. LEONATO

   Governor of Messina

6. RBOIAOCH = 6. BORACHIO

   He visits Margaret in the night to deceive Claudio.

7. ONTNES = 7. SONNET

   14 lined poem following ababcdcdefergg pattern

8. SDEOUNNEC = 8. DENOUNCES

   Upon hearing the accusations, Leonato ___ Hero as his daughter.

9. IMASENS = 9. MESSINA

   Setting of Much Ado

10. WOO =10. WOO

    Court with the intent to marry

11. OHNJ =11. JOHN

    Don Pedro's villainous brother

12. NCEKBIED =12. BENEDICK

    He is tricked into thinking Beatrice loves him.

13. ETCHAHOTO =13. TOOTHACHE

    Benedick blames his melancholy behavior on this.

14. ULED =14. DUEL

    Leonato challenges Claudio to one.

15. RGDBEOYR =15. DOGBERRY

    Constable of Messina

JUGGLE LETTER 2 Much Ado About Nothing

1. REATEIBC = 1. _____
She and Benedick have a love-hate relationship.

2. NOJH = 2. _____
Don Pedro's villainous brother

3. TRYAP = 3. _____
Leonato hosts a masquerade ____ at which the confusion in the play begins.

4. NFISAT = 4. _____
What Hero does after denying Claudio's accusations

5. SEERVG = 5. _____
Constable's assistant

6. OEOTNAL = 6. _____
Governor of Messina

7. MAELTN = 7. _____
Sad song of regret, usually for a lost love

8. WOO = 8. _____
Court with the intent to marry

9. LSNIUTS = 9. _____
Beatrice hurls these at Benedick upon his arrival.

10. ARIFR =10. _____
He devises the plan to restore Hero's reputation.

11. ELUD =11. _____
Leonato challenges Claudio to one.

12. ABAHSTRLA =12. _____
He sings the songs in the play.

13. NVAO =13. _____
Shakespeare's home: Stratford-Upon-___

14. LBKNA =14. _____
Unrhymed iambic pentameter: ___ verse

15. BORRGYDE =15. _____
Constable of Messina

JUGGLE LETTER 2 ANSWER KEY Much Ado About Nothing

1. REATEIBC = 1. BEATRICE
   She and Benedick have a love-hate relationship.

2. NOJH = 2. JOHN
   Don Pedro's villainous brother

3. TRYAP = 3. PARTY
   Leonato hosts a masquerade ____ at which the confusion in the play begins.

4. NFISAT = 4. FAINTS
   What Hero does after denying Claudio's accusations

5. SEERVG = 5. VERGES
   Constable's assistant

6. OEOTNAL = 6. LEONATO
   Governor of Messina

7. MAELTN = 7. LAMENT
   Sad song of regret, usually for a lost love

8. WOO = 8. WOO
   Court with the intent to marry

9. LSNIUTS = 9. INSULTS
   Beatrice hurls these at Benedick upon his arrival.

10. ARIFR =10. FRIAR
    He devises the plan to restore Hero's reputation.

11. ELUD =11. DUEL
    Leonato challenges Claudio to one.

12. ABAHSTRLA =12. BALTHASAR
    He sings the songs in the play.

13. NVAO =13. AVON
    Shakespeare's home: Stratford-Upon-___

14. LBKNA =14. BLANK
    Unrhymed iambic pentameter: ___ verse

15. BORRGYDE =15. DOGBERRY
    Constable of Messina

VOCABULARY RESOURCE MATERIALS

Much Ado About Nothing Vocabulary Word List

No.	Word	Clue/Definition
1.	ACCORDANT	Agreeable; compatible
2.	AGATE	Type of stone showing curved, colored bands or other markings
3.	ANGLING	Fishing with hook and line
4.	APPERTAIN	Belong as a part, right, possession, or attribute
5.	ARRAS	Wall hanging, as a tapestry
6.	BETROTHS	Promises to give in marriage
7.	BETWIXT	Between; in the middle
8.	CANKER	A fungal disease in plants or ulcer in animals; also, a variety of wildflower
9.	CAPON	Castrated male chicken
10.	CARPING	Petty fault-finding
11.	CATECHIZING	Instruction by means of question and answer
12.	CINQUEPACE	Lively dance, the steps of which were regulated by the number 5
13.	CLAMOR	Loud uproar, as from a crowd of people
14.	CODPIECE	Cover for the crotch in men's hose or tight-fitting breeches
15.	COMMODITY	Article of trade or commerce
16.	CONSTABLE	Officer of the peace having police and minor judicial functions
17.	COVERTLY	In a concealed, secret, or disguised manner
18.	COXCOMB	Vain and often foolish person
19.	COZENED	Misled by means of a petty trick or fraud; deceived
20.	CUCKOLD	Husband of an unfaithful wife
21.	CUDGELED	Struck or beat with a stick
22.	DAW	Simpleton; fool
23.	DEFILED	Made filthy or dirty; unclean
24.	DISDAINED	Regarded or treated with haughty contempt; despised
25.	DISPARAGE	Speak of or treat slightingly; depreciate; belittle
26.	DISSEMBLER	One who gives a false or misleading appearance
27.	DISSUADE	Advise or urge against
28.	DOTE	Bestow or express excessive love or fondness habitually
29.	DOUBLET	Close-fitting outer garment worn by men in the Renaissance
30.	ENFRANCHISED	Freed, as from bondage
31.	ENIGMATICAL	Perplexing; mysterious
32.	ENSUING	Following as a consequence or result
33.	EPITHET	Word or phrase applied to a person to describe an actual or attributed quality
34.	EXPEDIENT	Fit or suitable for the purpose; proper under the circumstances
35.	FLOUTING	Showing contempt for
36.	FOILS	Fencing swords having a circular guard and thin, flexible blades
37.	FOLLIES	Acts lacking good sense, understanding, or foresight
38.	FRAY	Noisy fight
39.	GALLANTS	Fashionable young men
40.	HAGGARDS	Adult hawks captured for training
41.	HAVOC	Great destruction or devastation; ruinous damage
42.	HEARKEN	Give heed or attention to what is said; listen
43.	HITHER	To or toward this place
44.	IMPEDIMENT	Obstruction; hindrance; obstacle
45.	INCITE	Stir, encourage, or urge on; stimulate or prompt to action
46.	INFAMY	Extremely bad reputation
47.	INTERMINGLE	Mix or become mixed together
48.	KNAVE	Unprincipled, untrustworthy, or dishonest person

Much Ado About Nothing Vocabulary Word List Continued

49.	LEAGUE	Unit of distance equal to 3.0 statute miles
50.	LECHERY	Unrestrained or excessive indulgence of sexual desire
51.	LIBERTINES	Those who act without moral restraint
52.	LIEGE	Feudal lord entitled to allegiance and service
53.	MALEFACTORS	Those who have committed a crime; criminals
54.	MANIFEST	Make clear or evident to the eye or the understanding
55.	MARL	Earthy mix of clay used as a fertilizer
56.	MELANCHOLY	Gloomy state of mind; depression
57.	MORTIFYING	Humiliating or shameful; hurting one's pride or self-respect
58.	OBSTINATE	Firmly or stubbornly holding to one's purpose or opinion
59.	OMINOUS	Portending evil or harm; foreboding; threatening
60.	ORTHOGRAPHY	The art of writing
61.	OSTENTATION	Conspicuous show or display intended to impress others
62.	PERADVENTURE	By chance; with doubt or uncertainty
63.	PERFUMER	One who makes or sells perfumes
64.	PERJURY	Willful giving of false testimony under oath
65.	PERNICIOUS	Causing harm or ruin
66.	PERTURBATION	Mental disquiet, disturbance, or agitation
67.	PESTILENCE	Deadly or virulent epidemic disease
68.	PIETY	The quality of being devoutly religious
69.	PLEACHED	Shaded or bordered with interlaced branches or vines
70.	PONIARDS	Daggers typically having slender square or triangular blades
71.	PRECEPTIAL	Procedural directive or rule
72.	QUALM	Sudden feeling of apprehensive uneasiness
73.	RECKONING	Settlement of accounts or of a score
74.	REDEMPTION	Being saved from error or evil
75.	RENDER	Provide; submit for inspection
76.	REPROVE	Criticize or correct
77.	REQUITED	Made a payment or return for
78.	SCRUPLE	Very small portion or amount
79.	SEDGES	Grass-like plants having solid stems, leaves in 3 vertical rows
80.	SEMBLANCE	Outward aspect or appearance
81.	SEXTON	Person employed to take care of a church
82.	SHREWD	Sharp or ill-tempered
83.	SIEVE	Perforated utensil used for straining or sifting
84.	SLANDERED	Made false and malicious statements or reports about someone
85.	SQUARER	Swashbuckler; one who delights in fighting
86.	TABOR	Small drum
87.	TARTLY	Sharply; in a cutting manner
88.	TEDIOUS	Boring, tiring, monotonous, dull
89.	THWARTING	Opposing and defeating the efforts, plans or ambitions of
90.	TRAVAIL	Painfully difficult or burdensome work; toil
91.	TURNCOAT	Person who changes to an opposing idea or reverses principles
92.	VALOR	Boldness or determination in facing great danger
93.	VARLET	Rascal; a knave
94.	VICTUAL	Food supply; provisions
95.	VOUCHSAFE	Allow or permit, as by favor or graciousness
96.	WANTON	Sexually lawless or unrestrained

VOCABULARY WORD SEARCH Much Ado About Nothing

```
Z R H C D S W R Y T E I P M L E A G U E
Y E E A O Q D F H M N S A P M D S P S Z
S N A T T U G W W F H N F D V J B E E F
N D R E E A A Y A R I H F F O Z V S D T
Y E K C T R L M E F A C I K R U Z T G W
H R E H T E Y W E V G H D T C E B I E B
P O N I A R D S D R A G G A H V T L S Q
A W N Z M V T I T V T L N B W E A E E K
R G G I T P D J O R E K O O S I R N X T
G L N N N Y E C X U E V E R T S T C T T
O I F G A R B D C R S D G P S B L E O K
H B T R D R X C I A Y D E L M C Y M N S
T E F F R R R L T M P C I M Y X I M L D
R R C L O K N A V E E O L Y P N B A E W
O T Q O C V B M S R F N N R O T N T T F
W I X U C W A O P B Y D T U L D I F I Q
R N G T A S C R U P L E S J E U M O C L
R E W I J L F O L L I E S R Q S A Y N G
D S P N Q M M C Y E H W E E L F R G I L
L X N G L I A V A R T D R P Z Y L K Y D
```

ACCORDANT	FRAY	MARL	SEDGES
AGATE	HAGGARDS	OMINOUS	SEXTON
ARRAS	HAVOC	ORTHOGRAPHY	SHREWD
CANKER	HEARKEN	PERJURY	SIEVE
CAPON	HITHER	PESTILENCE	SLANDERED
CATECHIZING	IMPEDIMENT	PIETY	SQUARER
CLAMOR	INCITE	PONIARDS	TABOR
DAW	INFAMY	PRECEPTIAL	TARTLY
DOTE	KNAVE	QUALM	TEDIOUS
DOUBLET	LEAGUE	REDEMPTION	THWARTING
FLOUTING	LIBERTINES	RENDER	TRAVAIL
FOILS	LIEGE	REQUITED	VALOR
FOLLIES	MANIFEST	SCRUPLE	VARLET

VOCABULARY WORD SEARCH ANSWER KEY Much Ado About Nothing

ACCORDANT	FRAY	MARL	SEDGES
AGATE	HAGGARDS	OMINOUS	SEXTON
ARRAS	HAVOC	ORTHOGRAPHY	SHREWD
CANKER	HEARKEN	PERJURY	SIEVE
CAPON	HITHER	PESTILENCE	SLANDERED
CATECHIZING	IMPEDIMENT	PIETY	SQUARER
CLAMOR	INCITE	PONIARDS	TABOR
DAW	INFAMY	PRECEPTIAL	TARTLY
DOTE	KNAVE	QUALM	TEDIOUS
DOUBLET	LEAGUE	REDEMPTION	THWARTING
FLOUTING	LIBERTINES	RENDER	TRAVAIL
FOILS	LIEGE	REQUITED	VALOR
FOLLIES	MANIFEST	SCRUPLE	VARLET

VOCABLUARY CROSSWORD Much Ado About Nothing

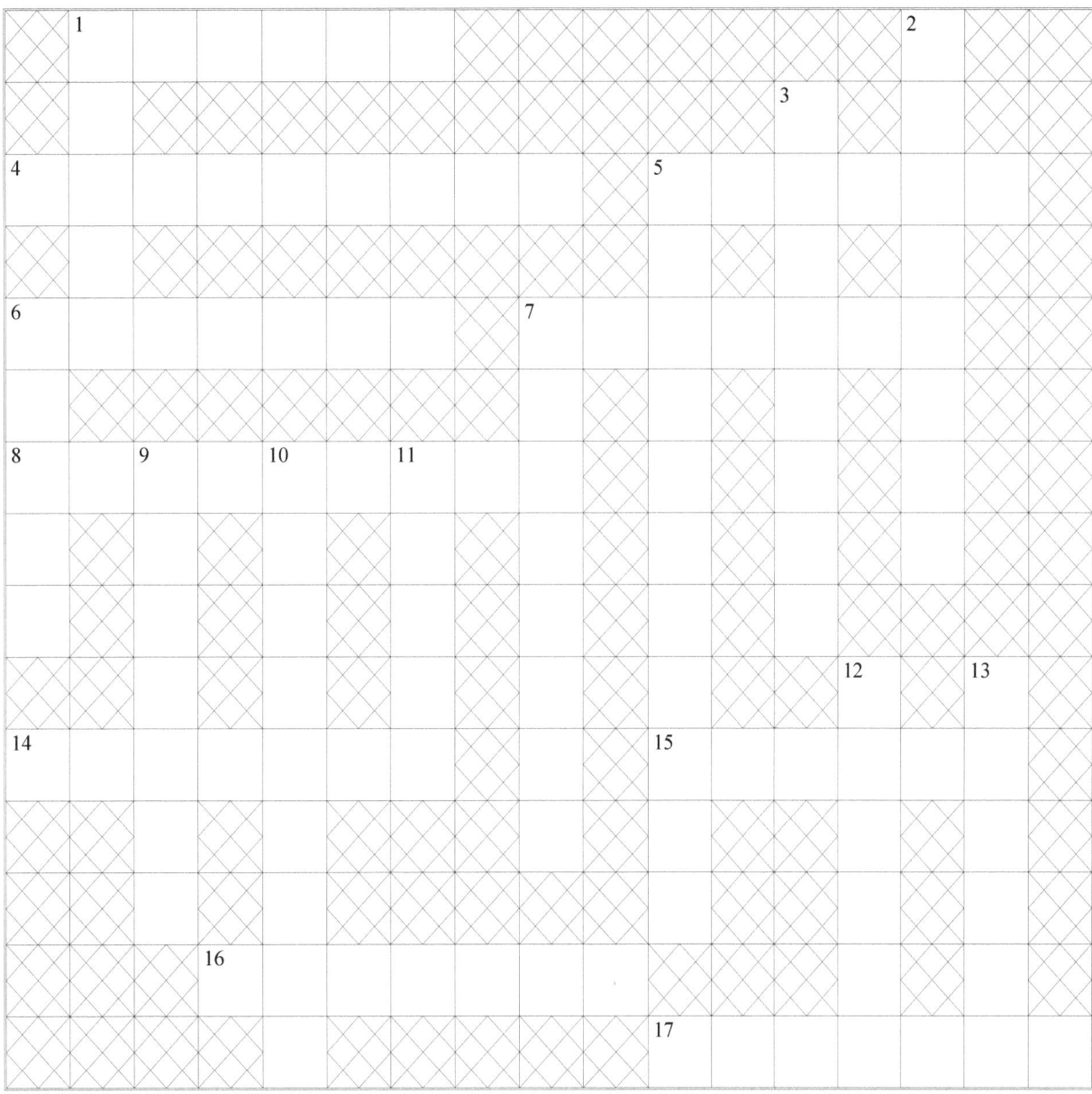

Across
1. A fungal disease in plants or ulcer in animals; also, a variety of wildflower
4. Belong as a part, right, possession, or attribute
5. Loud uproar, as from a crowd of people
6. Fishing with hook and line
7. Between; in the middle
8. Agreeable; compatible
14. Portending evil or harm; foreboding; threatening
15. Stir, encourage, or urge on; stimulate or prompt to action
16. Following as a consequence or result
17. Give heed or attention to what is said; listen

Down
1. Castrated male chicken
2. Showing contempt for
3. Make clear or evident to the eye or the understanding
5. Instruction by means of question and answer
6. Type of stone showing curved, colored bands or other markings
7. Promises to give in marriage
9. Petty fault-finding
10. Settlement of accounts or of a score
11. Wall hanging, as a tapestry
12. To or toward this place
13. Unit of distance equal to 3.0 statute miles

VOCABLUARY CROSSWORD ANSWER KEY Much Ado About Nothing

	1 C	A	N	K	E	R					2 F	
	A								3 M		L	
4 A	P	P	E	R	T	A	I	N	5 C	L	A	M	O	R
	O								A		N		U	
6 A	N	G	L	I	N	G	7 B	E	T	W	I	X	T	
G							E		E		F		I	
8 A	9 C	10 O	11 R	D	A	N	T		5 C		E		N	
T	A		E				R		H		S		G	
E	R		C				R		O		T			
	P		K		A		T		Z			12 H	13 L
14 O	M	I	N	O	U	S		15 I	N	C	I	T	E
			N		N			S		N		T	A
			G		I					G		H	G
				16 E	N	S	U	I	N	G		E	U
				G					17 H	E	A	R	K	E	N

Across
1. A fungal disease in plants or ulcer in animals; also, a variety of wildflower
4. Belong as a part, right, possession, or attribute
5. Loud uproar, as from a crowd of people
6. Fishing with hook and line
7. Between; in the middle
8. Agreeable; compatible
14. Portending evil or harm; foreboding; threatening
15. Stir, encourage, or urge on; stimulate or prompt to action
16. Following as a consequence or result
17. Give heed or attention to what is said; listen

Down
1. Castrated male chicken
2. Showing contempt for
3. Make clear or evident to the eye or the understanding
5. Instruction by means of question and answer
6. Type of stone showing curved, colored bands or other markings
7. Promises to give in marriage
9. Petty fault-finding
10. Settlement of accounts or of a score
11. Wall hanging, as a tapestry
12. To or toward this place
13. Unit of distance equal to 3.0 statute miles

VOCABULARY MATCHING 1 Much Ado About Nothing

___ 1. REPROVE
___ 2. DOUBLET
___ 3. SCRUPLE
___ 4. DEFILED
___ 5. LECHERY
___ 6. LIBERTINES
___ 7. ENIGMATICAL
___ 8. FLOUTING
___ 9. OBSTINATE
___ 10. TURNCOAT
___ 11. THWARTING
___ 12. FRAY
___ 13. ACCORDANT
___ 14. INFAMY
___ 15. PRECEPTIAL
___ 16. LEAGUE
___ 17. KNAVE
___ 18. IMPEDIMENT
___ 19. HAGGARDS
___ 20. CUCKOLD
___ 21. DISDAINED
___ 22. COZENED
___ 23. PLEACHED
___ 24. SHREWD
___ 25. PERJURY

A. Made filthy or dirty; unclean
B. Adult hawks captured for training
C. Extremely bad reputation
D. Those who act without moral restraint
E. Shaded or bordered with interlaced branches or vines
F. Showing contempt for
G. Perplexing; mysterious
H. Agreeable; compatible
I. Unit of distance equal to 3.0 statute miles
J. Willful giving of false testimony under oath
K. Person who changes to an opposing idea or reverses principles
L. Criticize or correct
M. Obstruction; hindrance; obstacle
N. Firmly or stubbornly holding to one's purpose or opinion
O. Very small portion or amount
P. Procedural directive or rule
Q. Noisy fight
R. Unrestrained or excessive indulgence of sexual desire
S. Sharp or ill-tempered
T. Misled by means of a petty trick or fraud; deceived
U. Unprincipled, untrustworthy, or dishonest person
V. Husband of an unfaithful wife
W. Regarded or treated with haughty contempt; despised
X. Opposing and defeating the efforts, plans or ambitions of
Y. Close-fitting outer garment worn by men in the Renaissance

VOCABULARY MATCHING 1 ANSWER KEY   Much Ado About Nothing

L - 1.	REPROVE	A. Made filthy or dirty; unclean
Y - 2.	DOUBLET	B. Adult hawks captured for training
O - 3.	SCRUPLE	C. Extremely bad reputation
A - 4.	DEFILED	D. Those who act without moral restraint
R - 5.	LECHERY	E. Shaded or bordered with interlaced branches or vines
D - 6.	LIBERTINES	F. Showing contempt for
G - 7.	ENIGMATICAL	G. Perplexing; mysterious
F - 8.	FLOUTING	H. Agreeable; compatible
N - 9.	OBSTINATE	I. Unit of distance equal to 3.0 statute miles
K -10.	TURNCOAT	J. Willful giving of false testimony under oath
X -11.	THWARTING	K. Person who changes to an opposing idea or reverses principles
Q -12.	FRAY	L. Criticize or correct
H -13.	ACCORDANT	M. Obstruction; hindrance; obstacle
C -14.	INFAMY	N. Firmly or stubbornly holding to one's purpose or opinion
P -15.	PRECEPTIAL	O. Very small portion or amount
I - 16.	LEAGUE	P. Procedural directive or rule
U -17.	KNAVE	Q. Noisy fight
M -18.	IMPEDIMENT	R. Unrestrained or excessive indulgence of sexual desire
B -19.	HAGGARDS	S. Sharp or ill-tempered
V -20.	CUCKOLD	T. Misled by means of a petty trick or fraud; deceived
W 21.	DISDAINED	U. Unprincipled, untrustworthy, or dishonest person
T -22.	COZENED	V. Husband of an unfaithful wife
E -23.	PLEACHED	W. Regarded or treated with haughty contempt; despised
S -24.	SHREWD	X. Opposing and defeating the efforts, plans or ambitions of
J - 25.	PERJURY	Y. Close-fitting outer garment worn by men in the Renaissance

VOCABULARY MATCHING 2 Much Ado About Nothing

___ 1. OBSTINATE
___ 2. COVERTLY
___ 3. LECHERY
___ 4. CODPIECE
___ 5. WANTON
___ 6. DISDAINED
___ 7. APPERTAIN
___ 8. VOUCHSAFE
___ 9. CUDGELED
___ 10. PESTILENCE
___ 11. CUCKOLD
___ 12. AGATE
___ 13. DOUBLET
___ 14. COZENED
___ 15. SHREWD
___ 16. DAW
___ 17. CLAMOR
___ 18. REPROVE
___ 19. INCITE
___ 20. SEDGES
___ 21. TEDIOUS
___ 22. DEFILED
___ 23. VICTUAL
___ 24. REDEMPTION
___ 25. LIBERTINES

A. Cover for the crotch in men's hose or tight-fitting breeches
B. Criticize or correct
C. Being saved from error or evil
D. Husband of an unfaithful wife
E. Food supply; provisions
F. Grass-like plants having solid stems, leaves in 3 vertical rows
G. Firmly or stubbornly holding to one's purpose or opinion
H. Regarded or treated with haughty contempt; despised
I. In a concealed, secret, or disguised manner
J. Belong as a part, right, possession, or attribute
K. Stir, encourage, or urge on; stimulate or prompt to action
L. Deadly or virulent epidemic disease
M. Misled by means of a petty trick or fraud; deceived
N. Unrestrained or excessive indulgence of sexual desire
O. Those who act without moral restraint
P. Made filthy or dirty; unclean
Q. Loud uproar, as from a crowd of people
R. Sexually lawless or unrestrained
S. Simpleton; fool
T. Boring, tiring, monotonous, dull
U. Close-fitting outer garment worn by men in the Renaissance
V. Struck or beat with a stick
W. Allow or permit, as by favor or graciousness
X. Sharp or ill-tempered
Y. Type of stone showing curved, colored bands or other markings

VOCABULARY MATCHING 2 ANSWER KEY Much Ado About Nothing

G - 1. OBSTINATE	A.	Cover for the crotch in men's hose or tight-fitting breeches
I - 2. COVERTLY	B.	Criticize or correct
N - 3. LECHERY	C.	Being saved from error or evil
A - 4. CODPIECE	D.	Husband of an unfaithful wife
R - 5. WANTON	E.	Food supply; provisions
H - 6. DISDAINED	F.	Grass-like plants having solid stems, leaves in 3 vertical rows
J - 7. APPERTAIN	G.	Firmly or stubbornly holding to one's purpose or opinion
W - 8. VOUCHSAFE	H.	Regarded or treated with haughty contempt; despised
V - 9. CUDGELED	I.	In a concealed, secret, or disguised manner
L -10. PESTILENCE	J.	Belong as a part, right, possession, or attribute
D -11. CUCKOLD	K.	Stir, encourage, or urge on; stimulate or prompt to action
Y -12. AGATE	L.	Deadly or virulent epidemic disease
U -13. DOUBLET	M.	Misled by means of a petty trick or fraud; deceived
M -14. COZENED	N.	Unrestrained or excessive indulgence of sexual desire
X -15. SHREWD	O.	Those who act without moral restraint
S -16. DAW	P.	Made filthy or dirty; unclean
Q -17. CLAMOR	Q.	Loud uproar, as from a crowd of people
B -18. REPROVE	R.	Sexually lawless or unrestrained
K -19. INCITE	S.	Simpleton; fool
F -20. SEDGES	T.	Boring, tiring, monotonous, dull
T -21. TEDIOUS	U.	Close-fitting outer garment worn by men in the Renaissance
P -22. DEFILED	V.	Struck or beat with a stick
E -23. VICTUAL	W.	Allow or permit, as by favor or graciousness
C -24. REDEMPTION	X.	Sharp or ill-tempered
O -25. LIBERTINES	Y.	Type of stone showing curved, colored bands or other markings

VOCABULARY JUGGLE LETTER 1 Much Ado About Nothing

1. DNETEPEIX = 1. _____
   Fit or suitable for the purpose; proper under the circumstances

2. SERIBESLMD = 2. _____
   One who gives a false or misleading appearance

3. LBUTODE = 3. _____
   Close-fitting outer garment worn by men in the Renaissance

4. ITYEP = 4. _____
   The quality of being devoutly religious

5. RAIETPNAP = 5. _____
   Belong as a part, right, possession, or attribute

6. OOCXMCB = 6. _____
   Vain and often foolish person

7. VHAOC = 7. _____
   Great destruction or devastation; ruinous damage

8. LATYRT = 8. _____
   Sharply; in a cutting manner

9. HSRTBETO = 9. _____
   Promises to give in marriage

10. HYRGPROOTHA =10. _____
    The art of writing

11. XENTSO =11. _____
    Person employed to take care of a church

12. PCCDOIEE =12. _____
    Cover for the crotch in men's hose or tight-fitting breeches

13. GALUEE =13. _____
    Unit of distance equal to 3.0 statute miles

14. SOIRPAND =14. _____
    Daggers typically having slender square or triangular blades

15. PACON =15. _____
    Castrated male chicken

VOCABULARY JUGGLE LETTER 1 ANSWER KEY Much Ado About Nothing

1. DNETEPEIX = 1. EXPEDIENT
Fit or suitable for the purpose; proper under the circumstances

2. SERIBESLMD = 2. DISSEMBLER
One who gives a false or misleading appearance

3. LBUTODE = 3. DOUBLET
Close-fitting outer garment worn by men in the Renaissance

4. ITYEP = 4. PIETY
The quality of being devoutly religious

5. RAIETPNAP = 5. APPERTAIN
Belong as a part, right, possession, or attribute

6. OOCXMCB = 6. COXCOMB
Vain and often foolish person

7. VHAOC = 7. HAVOC
Great destruction or devastation; ruinous damage

8. LATYRT = 8. TARTLY
Sharply; in a cutting manner

9. HSRTBETO = 9. BETROTHS
Promises to give in marriage

10. HYRGPROOTHA = 10. ORTHOGRAPHY
The art of writing

11. XENTSO = 11. SEXTON
Person employed to take care of a church

12. PCCDOIEE = 12. CODPIECE
Cover for the crotch in men's hose or tight-fitting breeches

13. GALUEE = 13. LEAGUE
Unit of distance equal to 3.0 statute miles

14. SOIRPAND = 14. PONIARDS
Daggers typically having slender square or triangular blades

15. PACON = 15. CAPON
Castrated male chicken

VOCABULARY JUGGLE LETTER 2 Much Ado About Nothing

1. XSOENT = 1. _____
   Person employed to take care of a church

2. AYLRTT = 2. _____
   Sharply; in a cutting manner

3. RTHHIE = 3. _____
   To or toward this place

4. RSAAR = 4. _____
   Wall hanging, as a tapestry

5. TIEIRBSLNE = 5. _____
   Those who act without moral restraint

6. ENSRADEDL = 6. _____
   Made false and malicious statements or reports about someone

7. RGDASIEAP = 7. _____
   Speak of or treat slightingly; depreciate; belittle

8. PRVEOER = 8. _____
   Criticize or correct

9. AVLETR = 9. _____
   Rascal; a knave

10. YORGIFINTM =10. _____
    Humiliating or shameful; hurting one's pride or self-respect

11. MENBALSCE =11. _____
    Outward aspect or appearance

12. ARNTITGHW =12. _____
    Opposing and defeating the efforts, plans or ambitions of

13. OOBXMCC =13. _____
    Vain and often foolish person

14. PTIXEEDEN =14. _____
    Fit or suitable for the purpose; proper under the circumstances

15. EEVSI =15. _____
    Perforated utensil used for straining or sifting

VOCABULARY JUGGLE LETTER 2 ANSWER KEY Much Ado About Nothing

1. XSOENT = 1. SEXTON
Person employed to take care of a church

2. AYLRTT = 2. TARTLY
Sharply; in a cutting manner

3. RTHHIE = 3. HITHER
To or toward this place

4. RSAAR = 4. ARRAS
Wall hanging, as a tapestry

5. TIEIRBSLNE = 5. LIBERTINES
Those who act without moral restraint

6. ENSRADEDL = 6. SLANDERED
Made false and malicious statements or reports about someone

7. RGDASIEAP = 7. DISPARAGE
Speak of or treat slightingly; depreciate; belittle

8. PRVEOER = 8. REPROVE
Criticize or correct

9. AVLETR = 9. VARLET
Rascal; a knave

10. YORGIFINTM =10. MORTIFYING
Humiliating or shameful; hurting one's pride or self-respect

11. MENBALSCE =11. SEMBLANCE
Outward aspect or appearance

12. ARNTITGHW =12. THWARTING
Opposing and defeating the efforts, plans or ambitions of

13. OOBXMCC =13. COXCOMB
Vain and often foolish person

14. PTIXEEDEN =14. EXPEDIENT
Fit or suitable for the purpose; proper under the circumstances

15. EEVSI =15. SIEVE
Perforated utensil used for straining or sifting

www.ingramcontent.com/pod-product-compliance
Lightning Source LLC
LaVergne TN
LVHW081532060526
838200LV00048B/2065